POLICY STUDIES IN EMPLOYMENT AND WELFARE NUMBER 5

General Editors: Sar A. Levitan and Garth L. Mangum

The Federal-State Employment Service A Critique

**Stanley H. Ruttenberg
and
Jocelyn Gutchess**

730150

The Johns Hopkins Press, Baltimore and London

The Johns Hopkins Press, Baltimore, Maryland 21218
The Johns Hopkins Press Ltd., London

Library of Congress Catalog Card Number 79-128824

ISBN 0-8018-1229-1 (clothbound edition)
      0-8018-1228-3 (paperback edition)

Originally published, 1970
Paperback edition, 1970

This book was prepared under a grant from The Ford Foundation.

Contents

List of Tables and Charts

CONTENTS

Preface

This book represents the second part of a three-part examination of our manpower institutions and their relation to social change. The first part deals with the overall structure within which manpower policy and programs operate, and has been published under the title *Manpower Challenge of the 1970s: Institutions and Social Change*. It includes an analysis of the development of manpower legislation during the past decade; a critical look at existing manpower planning and delivery systems; an expository account of the problems involved in setting up workable administrative machinery at the federal level; and a proposal for a model manpower system, as well as specifications for comprehensive manpower legislation geared to present day needs and goals.

In this second book we discuss the federal-state employment service, the manpower institution which has been a formidable roadblock to social change, but which we believe could be the key to the achievement of national manpower objectives. Rather than concentrate on the history of the employment service, or on a description of its function and purpose, we have tried to deal with it in terms of the major issues it faces today. Accordingly, this study stresses the effect of the reliance on the unemployment insurance tax; the competition with the unemployment insurance system; the lack of clearly defined purpose and goals; the administrative problems of planning and budgeting; the problem of state civil service systems; the inadequacy of training; and the influence of the Interstate Conference of Employment Security Agencies. Not content with calling the kettle black, we have suggested how it can be shined up and made new.

This study draws heavily on the experience and events between 1965 and 1969 when as Manpower Administrator and Assistant Secretary of Labor, I tried to get the employment service to redirect itself and develop a capability as the chief operating arm for national manpower policy. These efforts were not entirely successful, but I believe an important beginning was made.

Jocelyn Gutchess, my co-author, joins with me in expressing deep appreciation to Sar Levitan and Garth Mangum for their friendly comment and disciplined criticism which added focus and acuity to the study. We also express our thanks to Mrs. Ann Young, Mrs. Christine White, and Mrs. Gloria Scott for their help in the preparation of the manuscript.

The study was prepared under a grant from the Ford Foundation. In accordance with the Foundation's practice, complete responsibility for the preparation of the book was left to the authors.

STANLEY H. RUTTENBERG

The Federal-State Employment Service: A Critique

1

Introduction

Every government institution must be periodically subjected to a jolting reappraisal and overhaul to keep it in tune with changing national interests and priorities. Standing as it does at the center of our national manpower policy, the federal-state employment service is a prime candidate for such reappraisal.

As the oldest (37 years), largest (2,200 local offices), best equipped (35,000 people, $400 million annual budget), and only nationwide manpower service system, the federal-state employment service is the institution with the greatest potential for becoming the chief instrument for national manpower policy.[1] To fulfill that potential, it must develop a capability for flexible response to evolving national social and economic goals that, except in a few states, it does not now have.

Manpower policy operates on two fronts, the social and the economic. On the social front, it must assist individuals in the ful-

[1] Number of people estimated on basis of information supplied from the Department of Labor. During the fiscal year 1969, 30,400 state employment positions were supported from state grants funds. To this was added a conservative estimate of 5,000 positions funded from the more than $100 million allotted to the states from other sources such as MDTA, Job Corps, and WIN.

fillment of their working potential as well as in their adaptation to the world of work. In the 1960s this link with social policy demanded that we turn our attention to those left behind in the job world; to the disadvantaged.

Manpower policy is also a significant—in fact, an essential—element of the nation's economic policy. In periods of strong economic growth, manpower policy can act as a counter-inflationary force (1) through programs to bring the disadvantaged into the labor market, thereby increasing the total supply of trained labor and permitting employers to increase production of their products without having to bid up the price of labor; (2) by programs to ease skill shortage bottlenecks, thus relieving wage pressures; and (3) by improving the labor exchange, permitting a more efficient utilization of a limited labor supply. On the other hand, when the economy experiences a recession, manpower policy can provide a cushion protecting the economy against downward spiraling effects of layoffs.

The chief institution for implementing both aspects of manpower policy should be the federal-state employment service. It must always be ready and able to deal with the problems of structural unemployment, helping the disadvantaged prepare for and hold suitable jobs at decent wages. In addition, in times of large-scale unemployment, its chief concern must be to help place the mass of unemployed and assist in whatever public support programs are undertaken, including public works and other forms of public employment.

Despite tentative efforts over the past six years to become a catalyst in social change, above and beyond its more traditional role as a contributor to economic stability, the employment service has failed to develop the flexibility necessary to fulfill these dual roles. Although the employment service has generally met its objective whenever concentrating on the economic role, functioning more or less satisfactorily as a backstop for the free labor market, it has failed to achieve a proper balance between its economic and social roles.

As a manpower institution, the employment service has not been an effective agent for helping the disadvantaged. For many reasons—which will be discussed here—it has shown a lack of interest in helping the poor, a lack of imagination in meeting their problems, and an unwillingness to allocate resources to their needs. As a result, it is regarded by the poor and the disadvantaged as the least likely source of meaningful help, if not as the enemy; to be avoided at all costs.

The Nixon Administration has placed a high priority on manpower programs as a means to help people become productive and self-supporting. It has also been made clear that the employment service is expected to become the major instrument of national manpower policy. If this is to be the shape of the future, this is certainly the time for a critical look at the employment service, its problems, and its promise.

Whether the employment service *should* be the single agent for manpower policy might well be open to question; however, this study is intended to suggest *why* it has not filled its roles and why it cannot do so until basic changes are made in its mission and structure. The issue is simple. Can the employment service become a progressive organization capable not only of adjusting to change but also of promoting social and economic advancement? Or will it remain a barrier to progress, still performing the functions of another era and unable to meet the needs of today?

HISTORICAL BACKGROUND—THE ROOTS OF THE PROBLEM

Following the pattern of many government agencies, the employment service, which was established to fill a need created by one wave of social change, has turned into a breakwater against subsequent waves. By the early 1960s the employment service no longer saw itself in the forefront of the long struggle for achievement of goals of full employment and equal opportunity. Resistance to social change, not its support, seemed to demand the best talents and most creative energies of the staff. A brief look at some of the forces that have shaped this institution over its relatively short history may provide some clues as to how this situation came about.[2]

The federal-state employment service was established by the Wagner-Peyser Act of 1933, primarily to help the vast army of unemployed find jobs during the Great Depression. As it grew and became institutionalized during the 30s and 40s, three principal developments set a pattern that continues to influence its actions and reactions. They are (1) the basic funding arrangements; (2) the concept of universal service with its concomitant practice of screening the potential labor pool in behalf of employers; and (3) the dominance of the unemployment insurance system and its staff over the employment service and its functions.

The Wagner-Peyser Act called for a national system of state-administered employment offices supported by federal grants-in-aid on a matching basis.

The federal government would put up 50 percent of the funds from general revenues, and the states would put up the other 50 percent. It became apparent almost immediately that this matching procedure would not generate sufficient funds for the state employment services to perform the functions requested of them. The early years of the employment service were spent in a constant struggle merely to keep up with the stream of business: processing unemployment insurance claims and screening millions of unemployed for referral to public works and work relief projects. This huge job during the Depression put too much of a drain on state resources, so from the beginning, additional federal funds were tapped from programs like the National Youth Administration and the Civilian Conservation Corps.

The employment service was not limited for very long to general

[2] For a complete history of the development of the federal-state employment service, the reader is referred to William Haber and Daniel H. Kruger, *The Role of the United States Employment Service in a Changing Economy*, the W. E. Upjohn Institute for Employment Research, Kalamazoo, Mich., 1964, and Arnold Nemore and Garth Mangum, *Reorienting the Federal-State Employment Service*, the University of Michigan, Wayne State University, Detroit, 1968.

revenue funds. After two years of operation, it underwent a major change when, with the passage of the Social Security Act of 1935, a new concept of individual employment security was realized, embracing both employment service and unemployment insurance. The act placed the responsibility with the employment service for providing services to the unemployed under the new unemployment insurance system. With this responsibility came a new and stable funding resource. No longer were state offices completely dependent on the vagaries of the separate state legislatures. The Social Security Act linked the funding of at least one part of the employment service operations to a tax collected from employers.

During the war years (1942–46) when the employment service was federalized, all its funds came from appropriated general revenues. This precedent for 100 percent federal funding could not be turned aside when the federal government returned the employment service to the states in 1946. An amendment to the Wagner-Peyser Act in 1949 eliminated the matching provision and made all employment service funding a part of the social security system. Employment service operations were henceforth paid for from a federal unemployment insurance tax on employers, giving this group a special, if not privileged, interest in employment service administration.

Implicit in the Wagner-Peyser Act is the concept of a government-supported employment service as a primary adjunct of the labor exchange in a free economy. The provision of assistance to employers in their search for qualified workers is entirely consistent with this concept. However, since the employment service had to operate during the thirties and at frequent intervals after World War II in a situation of labor surplus and low labor demand, the need to entice employers to utilize its services inevitably became the prime focus of much of its effort. Local office staffs tended to refer only the best qualified applicants to fill job orders in the hope that employers would thus be encouraged to send in more job orders.

In time, this became the accepted practice. Even as late as

5

1964, in an official statement before the House Committee on Education and Labor, the Administrator of the Bureau of Employment Security (the federal agency charged with responsibility for the national employment security system, including both employment services and unemployment insurance) stated, "When an employer's choice is made from a *carefully screened* [italics provided] group of qualified applicants, the establishment will be staffed with more suitable workers and less subject to undesirable labor turnover."[3] "Screening" has remained a formidable obstacle to all efforts to shift the emphasis of the employment service in accordance with changing national needs.

The third development having a deep and lasting effect on the employment service has been its role in the administration of the unemployment insurance system. For many people the name "employment service" does not define sharply what functions are performed under its sign. The public often does not know whether a local employment service is intended to be an "unemployment" or an "employment" office. One reason for the confusion and ambiguity is the long-standing conflict within the employment security system—at both federal and state levels—as to what its proper mission should be; or at least which service—employment or unemployment insurance—should be given priority. During World War II, the duties of the employment service were clear; it was divorced from unemployment insurance and made the chief arm of the federal War Manpower Commission, with responsibility for seeing that national civilian manpower requirements were met. The concept of employment security took a back seat in the thinking of policy-makers, and gave way to the concept of manpower as a supply problem related to national security.

When the war ended, and returning veterans had been helped in their readjustment to civilian life, the employment service was returned to the states to again become a part of the employment security system. A struggle for ascendancy began between the

[3] U.S. Congress, House, *Hearings before the Select Subcommittee on Labor of the Committee on Education and Labor*, 1964, 88th Congress, 2nd Session, p. 166.

people concerned primarily with efficient administration of the unemployment insurance system and those primarily concerned with providing the kind of employment assistance necessary to improve the labor exchange. The series of recessions during the late forties and fifties favored the unemployment insurance system advocates, as employment service people were shifted to help with Unemployment Insurance System (UI) claims. A comparison of the workload of the two parts of the federal-state employment security system clearly shows that unemployment insurance has continued to dominate the work of local offices (Chart 1). Except for the war years and the 1946 bulge of veterans, the unemployment insurance system workload has always exceeded that of the regular employment service. This continuing predominance has had a significant impact on all phases of the employment service's operation and development.

The steady economic growth of the sixties which broke the previous pattern of repeated recessions, the civil rights movement, the concentration of government resources to eliminate poverty, and public recognition of the desperate situation of the cities, all led to new emphasis on federal manpower policy, an extensive array of new manpower programs, and new responsibilities for the employment service. But despite efforts during the Kennedy-Johnson years to bring about a redirection of the fifty state systems to meet these responsibilities, the necessary transformation of the employment service has not yet occurred.

When the system was first established it was intended to be a partnership with a strong national orientation. It has gradually become a confederacy of autonomous state agencies, each calling its own tune. National objectives cannot be achieved under such a system. If the federal government cannot retrieve its proper direction over the system—reasserting leadership, controlling resources, and setting priorities—the only alternative is federalization. Such a drastic step is neither necessary nor desirable, but time is fast running out when we can allow the states to dominate the partnership and frustrate national purpose.

A good example of the weakness of the federal partner in

7

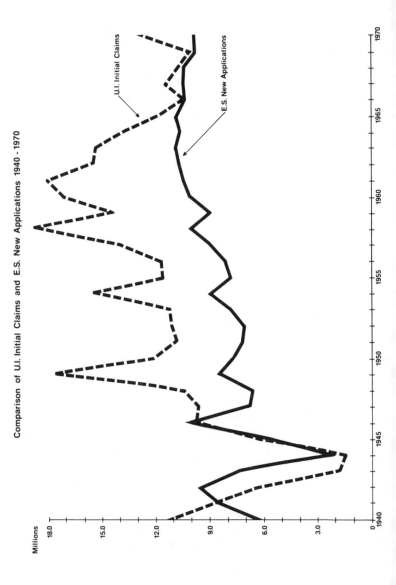

Comparison of U.I. Initial Claims and E.S. New Applications 1940 - 1970

bringing about reform within the state employment service system is the Human Resources Development Program, popularly known as HRD. This program (discussed in detail in Chapter 3) was intended to provide the means for the redirection of the employment service from its normal pursuits to providing intensive services to a new clientele, the disadvantaged.

The program was begun on a pilot basis in 1965 when reports on the characteristics of trainees in the Manpower Development and Training Act projects showed that the employment service was not reaching the hard-core unemployed.

Although there has been progress in some localities, there has not been the complete reorientation of staff that was hoped for. The consensus seems to be that, with the possible exception of Work Incentive Program (WIN), HRD is still more a paper program than a realistic description of local office operations.

Nevertheless, the concept of HRD is a good one. It makes sense. In WIN, where it has been given at least a trial, it is proving successful. The Nixon Administration has adopted HRD and is expanding the effort begun in 1966 to make it the standard operating procedure for local employment service offices. The effort will not succeed, however, unless there is a clear understanding of the causes that lie behind the intransigence and immobility of the employment service. A mountain cannot be moved without careful surveying and engineering. In the succeeding chapters, we shall analyze some of the problems that have all but frozen the employment service, examine the new developments which give promise of future reform, and suggest the steps that must be taken if the employment service is to fulfill its social and economic responsibilities to all who want to work, as well as to meet the manpower needs of our economy.

2

Barriers to Progress

The national concern of the sixties for the disadvantaged presented a radical challenge to the traditional role of the employment service and suggested that its mission ought to evolve from supplier or matcher of labor to developer of manpower. Legislation providing new manpower programs and resources gave the employment service the tools and resources necessary to carry out this new mission.

Starting with the Area Redevelopment Act and the Manpower Development and Training Act of 1962, and followed by the Economic Opportunity Act of 1964 and the 1967 amendments to the Social Security Act, there is now a broad range of manpower program authority to help those most in need to find and hold suitable employment.[1]

But the barriers to change within the employment service sys-

---

[1] For additional information on the development of manpower programs, the reader is referred to Sar A. Levitan and Garth L. Mangum, *Federal Training and Work Programs in the Sixties* (Ann Arbor: Institute of Labor and Industrial Relations, 1969), and Stanley H. Ruttenberg and Jocelyn Gutchess, *Manpower Challenge of the 1970s: Institutions and Social Change* (Baltimore: Johns Hopkins Press, 1970).

11

tem remain. In this chapter we have identified seven major institutional barriers to change. They are:

—the basic funding process which ties the employment service to the unemployment insurance system through a tax levied on employers;

—the dichotomy that exists between the Wagner-Peyser precept of universal service and the present day imperative to concentrate resources on those most in need of employment assistance;

—the built-in divisive contest between the unemployment insurance service and the employment service;

—the long-standing acceptance by both federal and state employment service staff of a body of established custom, prerogative, and procedure which frustrates federal direction whether through the budgetary process, or through other administrative devices;

—antiquated state civil service systems with inadequate or noncompetitive salary levels and stultified personnel policies;

—the abdication by the federal government to the states of responsibility for training of manpower staff; and

—the Interstate Conference of Employment Security Agencies, which from its unique position as a federally subsidized pressure group has presumed for itself a role in the operation of the national manpower program far beyond the usual concept of pressure politics in our democratic system.

While some of these impediments, as we have seen, are rooted in the historical development of the employment service, others are the result of individual prejudices and actions. Still others are due to institutional weaknesses in the federal-state system of government. An examination of the barriers and their causes should improve the chances for their removal.

FUNDING FACTS

Money may not be the root of all evil, but in this case it certainly contributes to the complexity of the problem. Unlike most federal-state programs which are financed by general revenue, the employment service gets its money from a special trust fund. This fund is patently inadequate, and its increase is limited by statute. Further, the special relationship of the employers who pay the tax which finances the employment service (ES) and the competition between the employment service system and the unemployment insurance system for limited revenue, all make the funding problem an overriding issue which must be resolved first and foremost.

The System—How It Works

Although other programs undoubtedly have equally complex funding problems, the intricacies of employment service financing seem quite unique. The taxing provisions operate in the following way:

The federal unemployment insurance tax is a payroll tax on most employers (some classes of employers are not covered under the law) presently set at 3.1 percent of the first taxable wages paid to (or earned by) a worker in a calendar year. States may have higher rates and/or a higher taxable wage base than the $3,000 federal standard, and some do, but these are the effective federal minimums. The tax is collected by the states for the federal government. The 3.1 percent tax is made up of two parts: a 2.7 percent tax which is used to pay individual insurance benefits and a .4 percent federal tax which is used to pay the costs of administering the unemployment insurance system, including the work test for insurance claimants *and other employment services.* As of May 1970, Congress had not completed action on a Nixon Administration proposal to raise the federal minimum rate to .5 percent, and the taxable wage base to $6,000. A similar proposal by the Johnson Administration was defeated.

When a state has an approved unemployment insurance law—as do all states as well as the District of Columbia, Puerto Rico, Guam, and the Virgin Islands—the tax payable to the federal government can be reduced by the amount that the employer has

13

paid under the state law. However, this reduction cannot be more than 2.7 percent. This leaves .4 percent which is always payable to the federal government and which is for the administration of the federal-state employment security system to fulfill its responsibilities under both the Social Security Act and the Wagner-Peyser Act.

Under its state law, each state is required to deposit the taxes it collects in the United States Treasury's Unemployment Trust Fund. Individual state's funds are kept separately, as is the .4 percent administrative fund.

Annual appropriations by the Congress are made from this administrative trust fund for employment security operations, including both the unemployment insurance system and the employment service system. These funds are called state grants.

Level of Funding: Inadequate Resources

Although the amount of money going to the states from the .4 percent administrative trust fund for the provision of employment services has tripled during the past decade—from $107 million in 1961 to an estimated $316 million in 1970—this still falls far short of the new demands put on the employment service. This is true despite the increasing proportion of the total state grant program going to the employment service—from 28 percent in 1961 to more than 50 percent this year. The proportion going to the states for the administration of the unemployment insurance system has decreased from 55 percent to 41 percent over the same period (Table 1).

The administrative expenses of operating the state employment service cannot be and are not being met by the .4 percent tax. To meet the demands that new manpower legislative programs have assigned to the employment service, as well as to finance the extra costs of providing service to the disadvantaged (who require more extensive and therefore more expensive help), the employment service has had to scrape and scrounge for additional revenue from other sources. For some years the trust fund revenues have

Table 1. Comparative Allocation of Trust Fund Grants to the States between the Unemployment Insurance Service and the Employment Service, 1955–70

(dollar figures in millions)

Year	Grants to States from Trust Fund Total	Amount Allocated for Administration of Unemployment Insurance Service[a]		Amount Allocated for Administration of Employment Service[a]	
	$	$	%	$	%
1955	193.5	124.8	65	68.1	35
1956	231.1	119.2	52	81.5	35
1957	248.0	131.4	53	85.3	34
1958	296.8	173.5	58	84.9	29
1959	305.5	176.9	58	94.9	31
1960	316.5	174.9	55	99.2	31
1961	378.5	207.1	55	107.6	28
1962	468.9	245.3	52	139.6	30
1963	407.0	226.0	56	155.5	38
1964	429.0	238.9	57	164.4	38
1965	438.2	234.8	54	181.4	41
1966	450.5	223.5	50	238.0	52
1967	520.5	232.3	45	264.5	51
1968	555.5	244.0	44	283.6	51
1969[b]	604.1	258.8	43	306.0	51
1970[b]	630.8	258.2	41	316.3	50

[a] Two categories of expenditures are now shown, administration and contingency. For this reason percentages do not add to 100 percent.

[b] Estimated.

been supplemented with funds from the Manpower Development and Training Act, the Economic Opportunity Act, Title IV of the Social Security Act (for the Work Incentive Program), and other appropriations to the Department of Labor. Table 2 shows the increase in the employment service budget from 1961 to 1970 and the extent to which the employment service has relied on non-trust account funds. It also exhibits the problems which would be posed by complete dependence on the unemployment insurance tax structure (Table 2).

In the past ten years funds from sources other than the trust fund have increased from 1 to 27 percent of total employment service revenues. As the Work Incentive Program grows and the employment service assumes more responsibility for other man-

15

Table 2. Employment Service Revenues, 1961–70

(in millions of dollars)

Fiscal Year	Total ES Revenues	Trust Fund, Grants to States ES only[a]	Non-Trust Fund Revenues						Non-Trust Fund Revenues (% of total)
			Total	MDTA	Job Corps	CEP	WIN	Others	
1961	107.6	107.6							
1962	140.8	139.6	1.2					1.2	1
1963	162.5	155.5	7.0	5.4				1.7	4
1964	174.6	164.4	10.2	8.1				2.0	5
1965	206.9	181.4	25.4	21.0	2.3			2.1	12
1966	261.9	236.0	25.8	17.8	4.0			3.9	9
1967	296.6	264.5	32.1	23.9	5.0			3.2	10
1968	337.9	286.6	51.2	38.2	6.9		.3	5.8	15
1969[b]	391.0	306.0	85.0	41.5	7.4	15.0	15.2	6.0	21
1970[b]	433.4	316.3	117.1	43.0	6.5	21.8	37.3	8.5	27

[a] Trust fund grants to the states for the administration of the unemployment insurance system are not included. See Table 1 for a breakdown of total state grants between ES and UI functions.

[b] Estimated. Totals may not add due to rounding.

power programs, this proportion can be expected to rise further. However, even this extra money is not enough to do the whole job. Money alone will not make the employment service completely efficient and responsive, but it is clear that the present level of funding does not match the size of the problem. The inadequacy is not limited to programs for the disadvantaged, but extends to other areas of employment service responsibility as well.

As one example: if the employment service is to fulfill its role in implementing national economic policy, a fully automated nationwide job matching system is required. Although no precise cost estimate can be made (an early estimate of $150 million for the installation of a national job matching system appears much too low), such a system could not possibly be financed from present employment service resources. Cost for the experimental job matching system presently under development in four or five areas is running higher than original estimates. Unforeseen problems in design and operation have arisen and new uses for the system have been developed.

Another example can be found in the employment service response to the needs of the unemployment insurance claimants. Since 1949, the employment service has been responsible for finding a suitable job for the UI claimant just as expeditiously as possible. In recent years, the claim has been made that unemployment insurance claimants are not getting the assistance they should. A 1968 survey in four cities appears to bear out this thesis.

Table 3 shows the results of that survey. "Nonexhaustees" are unemployment insurance claimants who were collecting unemployment compensation checks every week. The small proportion of nonexhaustees who receive any kind of assistance does not necessarily reflect good or bad administration, since most UI claimants have always found their own jobs. The figures serve only to provide a base line against which service to "Exhaustees," those whose benefit period has expired, can be measured. These people should be getting full support from the employment service but they got even less help than the nonexhaustees.

One way to increase services to unemployment insurance claim-

Table 3. **Employment Service Assistance to UI Claimants in Four Cities, 1968**
(percentages)

	Exhaustees	Nonexhaustees
Placed by ES	8	10
Counseled by ES	3	4
Tested by ES	2	2
Referred to training	2	1

SOURCE: Department of Labor, Manpower Administration, 1969.[2]

ants would be to utilize the trust fund account itself to pay for some of the manpower services that claimants need to get them back into the labor force as productive workers.

At the end of 1969, the trust fund reserves stood at over $12 billion, the highest in its history and more than 1.5 times the highest annual cost level during the past ten years. This money could be put to work to help those it was intended to help, providing special training where necessary to equip them to become full-time workers again. Such a proposal usually evokes a strong reaction from employer and state interests.

It is argued that the trust funds are inviolate because they belong to the states and not to the federal government, that the funds are just another part of the national debt—owed by the federal government to the states. Following this line of argument, federal direction as to how the funds should be used is considered an unjustified instrusion of the federal government into state affairs. This belief is strongly held by many of those who work in the field of unemployment insurance and presents a stubborn barrier to an effective linking of the unemployment insurance program to a flexible economic policy. And yet, the system could, and ought to be, one of the most efficient and versatile tools available for implementation of national economic policy.

If the state share of the trust fund is inviolate, then we must rely on the federal share. But the tax of .4 percent of the first $3,000 of wages simply does not produce enough revenue to permit the employment service to do the job that is expected of it. Until

[2] U.S. Department of Labor, Bureau of Employment Security, Unemployment Insurance Service, unpublished data, November 14, 1968.

the tax is raised (as it was in 1961, from .3 to .4 percent) or the taxable wage base increased, or both, the financial bind will become tighter each year, forcing federal administrators to devise more clever and inventive ways of keeping the employment service solvent. The proposal enacted in September 1969 putting the collection of federal unemployment taxes on a current basis represents such an effort.[3] However, this device has limited use. Advancing the date of tax collection produces a temporary abatement, but cannot postpone forever the day of reckoning.

Source of Funds: The Employer

When the employment service was established in 1933, it was intended to serve the public and to be administered in the general public interest. However, it is paid for by a tax levied only on employers, whose interests are not always synonymous with the general interest. The obligation to pay the .4 percent payroll tax to the federal government gives employers a direct concern with the operations as well as the costs of the employment service. It can be reasonably assumed that an employer would rather not have that tax increased to .5 percent or .6 percent unless it can be shown that the increase will be proportionately beneficial to him.

Employers' proprietary interest in the employment service is further enhanced by the experience rating system. This system permits an employer to reduce his tax—not the .4 percent, but the 2.7 percent or more that he pays for unemployment insurance —if he is a "good" employer, that is, one who does not cause unemployment. The theory behind the unemployment tax system is that the insurance program should be as much an unemployment preventative as a temporary means of support for the worker who becomes unemployed through no fault of his own. The system assumes employer responsibility for unemployment, with the con-

[3] The proposal to put the FUTA tax collection on a current basis was originally included in the Johnson budget submission for the fiscal year 1970. It was retained by the Nixon Administration primarily because the existing financial crisis left no choice.

comitant proposition that an employer who does not cause unemployment should be recognized and rewarded.

Since the experience rating already gives the employer some degree of control over his tax rate, it may also contribute to a disposition on the part of employers to regard the federal share of the tax within a very narrow definition.

The argument is often put forth that the proceeds of the .4 percent tax should not be used to provide manpower services that are not directly related to the operation of the unemployment insurance system. Those who hold this view concede that the regular employment service operations are a basic part of the overall employment security system. However, opposition is strong in many quarters to the use of the trust fund account for employment service programs such as certification of alien workers and employers under the Immigration and Naturalization Act, agricultural recruitment and placement activities, and programs for young workers entering the labor force, on the grounds that none of these groups is covered under the unemployment insurance system.

A registered lobbying group, the Unemployment Benefit Advisors, Inc., effectively protects the interests of the employers in keeping the tax down. Started in Wisconsin when that state enacted the first unemployment insurance legislation, the original purpose of the organization was to provide employers with forms and accompanying instructions to comply with the new tax and new program. When Congress enacted the Federal Unemployment Insurance Law in 1937 (Title III of the Social Security Act), the Benefit Advisors moved to Washington to perform similar services for employers on a national scale.

Today instruction to employers about forms is no longer required, but the protection of employer interests in Washington and in state capitols is a very salable service which the Benefit Advisors perform with singular effectiveness. Although it is a relatively small organization, and charges minimal fees, the Benefit Advisors is influential and successful in achieving its objective:

low taxes. The organization is strong not because of who they are, but because of whom they represent.

UNCERTAIN MISSION—EMPLOYMENT SERVICES FOR WHOM?

One of the most persistent roadblocks to a responsive, progressive employment service is the continuing and fundamental difference of opinion as to what its mission should be. Should it be a comprehensive public service available to every and any person who wants employment assistance, or should it be the operational tool of national manpower policy? It cannot be both without the expenditure of a very large amount of money.

The Case for Universal Service

Those who argue for universal service find justification in the language of the Wagner-Peyser Act of 1933. Section 3(a) of that act states: "It shall be the province and duty of the [United States Employment Service] to promote and develop a national system of employment offices for men, women, and juniors who are legally qualified to engage in gainful occupations. . . ." This is interpreted to mean that the employment service cannot legally turn anyone away.

Mr. Robert Goodwin, former Administrator of the Bureau of Employment Security, stated the position well when testifying before the House Appropriations Committee in March 1965. He was asked why the employment service did not charge a user fee to employers since the services that were being performed were "so valuable." He replied:

I suppose that would be possible. We think that employers are as much entitled to these services as are the workers. We would see no more reason for the establishment of a fee with respect to services for the local employment office than there would be in a school system or some other similar service. *In other words, this is a basic service that the Government has decided should be available to all people.* [Italics provided.] It is optional; people can use it or not use it. But it is a very basic service in helping people to get employment and help-

21

ing employers with some of their problems. We do not think it would be advisable to institute a fee. It has been considered . . . but we have concluded it is not desirable.[4]

Supporters of universal service concede that there could be some flexibility in the kinds of clients that the employment service should seek, concentrating on the disadvantaged in periods of prosperity—but they argue that the shift in emphasis should never be all the way. To abandon completely the capacity for service to all, they contend, would sacrifice the ability of the employment service to shift back again as the national employment picture changed. Three reasons are usually given:

—personnel cannot be shifted easily to new duties;
—neighborhood offices are not easily relocated;
—a clientele of employers is built up slowly, after careful cultivation of working relationships and provision of satisfactory service. If not satisfied, the employers will withdraw their business, place the job orders elsewhere, and will not be apt to return.

Following this line of argument, maintenance of a permanently flexible posture requires the retention of at least a minimum capacity to serve all groups, including professional workers.

In the late 50s and 60s, the employment service made a strenuous effort to improve its capacity for universal service by introducing industrial-occupational grouping in its offices that paralleled the labor market. Outlying neighborhood offices were closed down and separate offices were established for occupational groups: clerical and sales, manufacturing, professional, casual labor, and domestic services. The new offices were established in areas within easy reach of employers normally hiring a given group (e.g., the office specializing in manufacturing was placed near industrial plants). All of this was done in a deliberate attempt to convince both employers and workers that the employ-

[4] U. S. Congress, House, Subcommittee of Committee on Appropriations Hearings, *Appropriations for the Department of Labor for 1966*, 89th Congress, 1st Session 1965, pp. 298–99.

ment service was the best place for each to solve his employment problems.

These changes in the operating structure of the employment service completely prepared it to perform what became its predominant function—placement. Almost all staff energy was directed toward carrying out the labor exchange function with maximum efficiency. The preceding decade of repeated recessions, and the belief that an improved labor market exchange was a significant anti-recession measure, provided justification for this new orientation.

After 1961 when the nation began a period of steady economic growth, social priorities changed. The problems of the poor and the disadvantaged—particularly with regard to jobs and employment—appeared in stark contrast to the general prosperity of most of the work force. The government could not disregard them. All of this dictated an entirely different manpower policy—one which made the concept of universal service hard to justify.

THE EMPLOYMENT SERVICE—UNEMPLOYMENT INSURANCE CONTEST

The continuing contest for ascendancy between the two parts of the employment security system—the employment service and the unemployment insurance service—is another divisive and debilitating force. This contest manifests itself in the recurrent debate on separation of the two services, the differences that typify the separate staffs, the leadership of state employment security agencies, and even the structural organization of the system at every level: federal, state, and local.

In most states (excepting only Arizona, Hawaii, Wisconsin, and the District of Columbia) both the employment service and the unemployment insurance functions are jointly administered by a single state body—the employment security agency. However, actual operations of the two services are usually kept separate. The two staff groups go their separate ways, performing different functions and serving, to some extent, different clienteles. Over the years, each service has developed its own esprit and identity. Each attracts a distinct kind of staff, and those distinctions have long been reinforced by state civil service requirements. State merit system qualifications for a position in the unemployment insurance service generally include accounting, financial or clerical experience, or a similar type of education. The journeyman in the UI system is a claims examiner. The employment service, on the other hand, calls for people with backgrounds in personnel work or vocational guidance. The ES journeyman is an employment interviewer. The difference in background is reflected in the different approach and outlook that each group brings to its job. UI people generally see themselves as guardians and protectors of a financial system which would be an easy mark for cheating or exploitation if it were not for their careful scrutiny of all transactions. Employment service people are more likely to have an image of themselves as defenders of individuals, as protagonists for those who need employment assistance and cannot get it elsewhere.

The inherent rivalry between the two agencies was heightened by a series of organizational moves which alternately kept them apart or pulled them together. Starting the course unevenly (the employment service was established first, the unemployment insurance service two years later) the two services were together until World War II brought federalization to the ES and left UI with the states.

For the UI, this separation intensified the division that already existed. Here was the employment service actively engaged in supporting the war effort, while unemployment insurance personnel were left behind with little or nothing to do. When the war ended and the employment service returned to the states, the seniority that unemployment insurance people had gained by remaining with the state civil service systems put them in command of the revived state employment security agencies. In addition, the cycle of recessions in the fifties placed a greater workload on UI, causing employment service people to be pulled into unemployment insurance work. This situation helped UI leadership maintain its ascendancy. Evidence of that ascendancy is easily found today in the upper-level staff of most state employment security agencies.

State administrators come from all walks of life and represent widely differing backgrounds, but the largest and most influential single group are those who have worked up through the ranks of the employment security system, more often than not on the unemployment insurance side. The next largest group of state administrators came to their jobs with a background in business, usually small business.[5] Together, the old line administrators and employers-turned-public executives form a powerful alliance whose primary interest is in the insurance rather than the employment service aspect of employment security and whose natural instinct is for thrift and economy first, service second.

A more decisive factor contributing to the conservatism of state agency leadership is the political character of many of the state appointments. Even when appointments are not subject to the pleasure of individual state governors, state administrators generally have strong political ties within the state which give them a degree of immunity to direction from Washington.

Whether it is because of long association with UI, previous affiliation with the business interests, or political expendiency, it has been apparent for some time that state administrators as a group have shown less interest in improvements in the employment service than in the management of the unemployment system. One official, long in UI, explained why he felt that his program should take precedence over the employment service. He maintained that UI was the real world, where there could be an effect on public policy, especially on economic policy, whereas he considered ES merely a management problem.[6]

As long as the employment service is dominated by men and women whose motivation and interest is antithetical, or at least unsympathetic, to the employment service function, the capability

[5] Information on the backgrounds of state employment security administrators taken from a survey conducted by the Interstate Conference of Employment Security Agencies in January 1969.

[6] Interview with Forest L. Miller, at that time Acting Director of the Unemployment Insurance Service, March 1969.

25

of the employment service for radical self-reform remains dubious.

The contest between the employment service and unemployment insurance service is not confined to differences in staffs or the interests of the leadership. It can also be seen in the way employment security functions are organized. The issue of separation is more than an exercise in administrative management. It involves questions of policy and program emphasis.

Under the employment security concept, the two functions are closely related. Employment security starts with the individual worker and his employment-related needs. If he wants to work, he should have a job commensurate with his skills and aptitudes. If he wants to work but cannot because he is inadequately prepared or because of institutional barriers, he should be given assistance in becoming prepared and overcoming the barriers. If he loses his job through no fault of his own, he should be given financial support while he is out of work and helped to find and hold another job. Unemployment insurance and manpower service are two faces of the same problem. The employment service must, of course, provide manpower services, including the work test, to unemployment insurance claimants. It must also contribute to the smooth working of the labor market, in order to help maintain a favorable economic climate which will result in lower unemployment rates, thus enchancing employment security for all workers.

There can be no doubt that the relationship between the two services is a close one. It does not necessarily follow that to sustain that relationship there must be a single unified administration. Coordination: yes. Monolithic organizational structure: no.

In the early sixties, the states were instructed to make a physical separation of the two functions in the expectation that such a division would improve the image of the employment service. It was thought that neither good employers nor good workers would use the employment service office because of its identification with the unemployed—those who in the public eye were usually viewed as less desirable workers. Today, it is not the image with employers that is important. The overriding issue is how well the employment service can serve those who need help most, and at the same time effectively complement the work of the unemployment insurance service, as both agencies work toward achievement of the national goal of full employment. Whether coordination between the two services requires unified administration at the state and local level, or whether it can be achieved through some other coordinating mechanism has yet to be resolved.

At the federal level, separation of the operations of the two services was achieved in the reorganization of the Manpower Administration of the Department of Labor. The Bureau of Employment Security which formerly handled both functions was abolished. Two new offices were established, the Unemployment Insurance Service and the United States Training and Employment Service (USTES). The latter has operating responsibility for manpower work and training programs as well as basic employment services normally provided by the federal-state employment service. Policy and program coordination is accomplished through the Manpower Administrator, to whom both services report. Regional manpower offices replicate the division between UI and USTES, with both services reporting to a Regional Manpower Administrator. As far as the financing is concerned, the division between trust fund management and general revenue management has been maintained.

If the federal government has a single administrative structure at the head of the Manpower Administration, should not the states also have a single focus of control? Does not the argument for separation of the two functions fall apart in the face of the federal example of the Manpower Administration? The argument holds if a clear distinction is made between operations and staff activities. The important thing is to make sure that one set of interests does not dominate the other—in this case, that unemployment insurance interests not continue to dominate employment service interests.

27

Federal Control through the Budget Process

Through adroit management of the power of the purse, a program administrator can gain firm control over the budgetary process and the allocation of funds, and thereby exert enough force to counteract institutional rigidity. That is the theory, but with the employment service, despite repeated attempts, gaining control has proved difficult and elusive. In a federal-state program, control over the allocation of federal funds can be exercised at several points in the budgetary process: at the beginning, when initial state spending plans are submitted and approved; in the middle, when adjustments are made to balance requirements against actual congressional appropriations; and at the end, when there is an opportunity to reward or punish performance through control of the budget for the following year.

During the sixties, the effort to gain control of the employment service budget involved at least three different approaches: direct intervention in the budget process; reform of the basic employment service legislation; and the introduction of modern management techniques, particularly in planning and budgeting. The effort was hampered by several factors, some based on law, and some due to long established custom. The Attorney General has ruled that once federal dollars have been turned over to a state and deposited in its account, the money belongs to the state, and the federal government must relinquish control over its expenditure. The logical concomitant of this ruling is that the federal government cannot reclaim funds it has relinquished to the states, except under conditions previously agreed to by both parties. Nor can it withhold some portion of funds which have been apportioned to the states because of inadequate or poor performance. In the case of employment security trust funds, the only sanction available to the federal government is to close down state employment service and unemployment insurance operations completely. Since such a course is unthinkable, for all practical purposes the options for the federal government are nonexistent. The only effective weapon left to the administrator in this situation is the review of state plans *before* the apportionment to the state is made.

For many years, state employment service agencies have prepared annual state plans which formed the basis for allocation of funds from the trust fund account. These plans projected the state agency's operations for the year in terms of work-load-unit time categories: for example, so many counseling interviews, so many placements, so many tests given. These work-load-units were then translated into required positions, the positions added up and multiplied by the appropriate salary figures, and the plan finished. When it was sent to Washington for review, there was no way to accurately assess the plan since it bore no particular relation to local needs, nor could the assumptions on which it was made be tested for relevance to the clients to be served. Indeed, since the plans emphasized the ratio of placements to applicants as a justification for increased state agency staff, the system guaranteed that the disadvantaged, those least easily placed, would be shunted aside in favor of the easy to place, those who needed help least. Once the plans were approved, they became almost sacrosanct and any redirection during the year became difficult, if not impossible.

The 1966 Budget Increase—An Attempt at Direct Intervention

It was clear that if the employment service were to become responsive to social needs and problems, this planning system with its cursory review followed by virtual surrender of control over program administration, would have to be revised. The first venture into this important area began with the presentation of the fiscal year 1966 budget to the Congress in March 1965. Included in the budget were two items specifically designed to carry out the Johnson Administration policy in two high priority areas—youth unemployment and urban ghetto unemployment.

The first item was a $37 million request to establish Youth Opportunity Centers (YOC)—separately identified employment service offices in metropolitan areas to assist unemployed youth. Work-

29

ing closely with community action agencies (CAA) and using trained youth counselors and other supportive personnel, the centers were especially designed to help young people in the difficult transition from school to work. Since this $37 million was to be drawn from general revenue funds, it was susceptible to tighter federal control than funds appropriated from the trust fund account.

Congress appropriated $10 million of the $37 million requested. Then, unfortunately, the entire program was dropped in one of the Johnson economy drives, so the experiment with controlled general revenue funds for specific employment service operations was never tested.

The second budgetary issue that later became the source of considerable conflict between the Manpower Administration and the state agencies was over $10 million to be appropriated from the trust fund: $7.5 million for improvement in basic employment services to the disadvantaged in major metropolitan areas, and $2.5 million for staff training and executive development. The congressional justification for the increase stated clearly that the money was to be used to take care of the additional workload caused by "the need for specialized services of major and growing segments of the workforce (other than youth) especially older workers and minority groups."[7] Additional funds were needed because the group that the employment service would be dealing with were harder to help than the people it had previously served.

The statistics measure the number of people who receive service, however, they give no indication of the number of job seekers who receive little or no service beyond the acceptance of an application or receive service inadequate for their needs. This consideration applies with particular force to the disadvantaged youth, older workers, minorities, the handicapped and those with obsolescent skills who require intensive services, especially counseling, training and job development, in order to obtain suitable employment.[8]

[7] U. S. Congress, House, Subcommittee of the Committee on Appropriations Hearings, *Appropriations for the Department of Labor for 1966*, 89th Congress, 1st Session 1965, p. 324.

[8] *Ibid.*, p. 337.

Similarly, the money requested for training state agency personnel was justified on the basis that the new programs—aimed primarily at the disadvantaged—required a new and different emphasis on staff development.

Congress was persuaded and appropriated the full amount from the trust fund account. To assure that the funds were actually used for the intended purposes, the Manpower Administration put the money into reserve until detailed plans for its use were drawn up by the states and submitted for approval. The Bureau of Employment Security—reacting in predictable fashion—wanted an across-the-board distribution of the funds to all states using normal apportionment formulas. Even with a judicious distribution, the effect would have been a diffusion of impact, and very likely no significant improvement in services to the disadvantaged. National manpower policy was committed to assisting the areas and groups most in need of employment help. If the federal government, represented by the Manpower Administration, did not insist on detailed plans for these extra funds, it would forfeit the right and the opportunity to effectively carry out that commitment.

Throughout the fall and early winter, the struggle within the Manpower Administration continued, with the Bureau of Employment Security pushing hard for a general distribution and the Manpower Administration holding fast to the requirement for detailed plans for specific programs before releasing the funds. Such plans were eventually submitted, but they were couched in general terms. They were inexact in naming specific local offices where the money would be used and vague as to purpose. By the end of the year, funds for staff development had been released, but the balance was never fully utilized as intended.

This particular bureaucratic struggle, insignificant as it may seem, illustrates how pervasive the resistance to change in the employment service was, and how effective it could be in frustrating national purpose, even when the amount of money involved was relatively inconsequential in terms of the employment service budget (which that year totaled approximately $220 million).

The Manpower Services Act of 1966

Since the effort to force change by control of the budget and allocation of resources succeeded only in engendering the hostility of the state agencies without making any significant constructive impact on the system, the next recourse was the legislative route.

In October 1965, Secretary of Labor Willard Wirtz appointed a task force "to review the operations of the employment service and to consider what is needed to improve its operations as the front-line agency for translating manpower education and training and war on poverty into operational reality."[9] The task force was chaired by Nixon's first Secretary of Labor, Dr. George P. Shultz, then the Dean of the Graduate School of Business at the University of Chicago. The vice chairman was Dr. Arnold Weber, Manpower Assistant Labor Secretary under Shultz, but at that time a professor at the University of Chicago. In its report the task force recommended that part of the employment service budget be drawn from general revenue funds. It was clear that the task force had in mind particularly those services performed by the employment service as a part of the national manpower program but not directly related to the administration of the unemployment insurance system. It also recommended that the budget and planning process then in force be changed to reflect program goals, and thereby become an administrative tool which could be used to implement national policy decisions.

A bill embodying these and other task force recommendations was introduced in Congress by Senator Joseph Clark and Congressman Elmer Holland, both of Pennsylvania. The Clark-Holland Manpower Services Act included an item veto provision, giving the Secretary of Labor authority to withhold a part of a state's allocation of funds instead of the existing all or nothing sanction.

The Senate passed this bill in June 1966, but amendments added

[9] Secretary of Labor Willard Wirtz, in a directive announcing appointment of a Task Force to Review the Operations of the Federal-State Employment Service, October 1965. The Report of the Task Force, which was unanimous, was issued on December 23, 1965.

on the floor so weakened it that enthusiasm for proceeding was seriously undermined. As a result, the emasculated version was allowed to die in the House Committee. It should be noted that the Senate amendments were not directed at the budgeting and allocation process, but at the issue of federal standards for state personnel. In addition, through an unfortunate misunderstanding, the entirely unrelated issue of employment service involvement in agricultural strikes was permitted to become intermingled with the bill, with the result that vital union support was lost.

The Introduction of a Modern Management System

With the probability of effecting change by federal directive seriously weakened by entrenched bureaucratic interests, and with the possibility of legislative relief deferred, if not eliminated entirely, there was still another administrative route to bring about change: to modernize the planning and budgeting process of the employment service. Although such a course did not demand special legislation, it did require a break in the long-established interdependency between the Bureau of Employment Security and the state agencies. A change in the leadership of the employment service could help to foster such a break. For some time effective leadership had been frustrated, hemmed in as it was by established procedures and traditional relationships.

Under Mr. Frank Casscll, who took leave from his job in private industry from March 1966 to September 1967, and Mr. Charles Odell, who succeeded Cassell, the employment service took the first steps toward a management system that could be used as an instrument for change. Development of the proposal that was adopted had begun under Mr. Louis Levine, Cassell's predecessor. It included four basic elements: (1) an operating plan or plan of service, (2) an applicant-oriented reporting system, (3) continuous monitoring of state and local operations, and (4) an evaluation system to measure the results of service instead of

33

levels of activity. Although skeptics within the Bureau of Employment Security argued that the federal government would never be able to follow through with the careful monitoring and evaluation necessary to make the system work, the proposal was adopted. It was even accepted by the states without opposition, probably because they felt that such a course could avert federal interference in the conduct of their affairs.

The plan of service procedure was initiated with the fiscal 1968 budget cycle. Applying modern management techniques to the employment service program, the plan of service requires a definition of the problem to be solved, the setting of incremental objective goals in meeting the total problem, an assessment of all available resources and their potential for meeting the goals, consideration of alternative methods of achieving the objective goal, and the establishment of an order of priority related to local needs and consistent with national policy.

Planning was to start with each local area office's examining its own manpower needs and resources. From this assessment the local area would indicate how it planned to meet those needs, where services would be performed, who would be served, and in what way. If it was demonstrated, through monitoring and evaluation, that the services being performed were not producing the desired results, the federal government would have a basis for enforcing changes when the plan came up for renewal the next year. An item veto could be exercised in advance of allocation of resources. For the first time, the federal government would have an effective management tool to bring about institutional change responsive to national objectives. In effect, the federal government was saying to the states: tell us in objective terms what you expect to achieve, and if your goals are consistent with national policy, we will give you the money to do the job. How you go about achieving the desired results is your business, but *you will be judged on results, not activities.*

The first real test of the new system came in 1968 when the employment service faced a reduction in appropriations for 1969: a 10 percent cut in Manpower Development and Training Act

34

funds paid to the employment service to select trainees for MDTA training, refer them to such training, and follow up on them after they leave training; and a 3 percent cut in funds from the trust fund account. An *ad hoc* committee of the Interstate Conference of Employment Security Agencies (ICESA) was called by the Bureau of Employment Security (BES) to discuss how the decrease should be administered. The committee wanted the cut applied across-the-board as it had been two years earlier. When the fiscal year 1967 BES appropriation was reduced by Budget Bureau action at that time, the BES prevailed and there was a general reduction of employment service activities. No single ongoing employment service program or agency suffered unduly, but the opportunity to use the cut to exercise federal control and force changes in the employment service operations was sacrificed. To allow the fiscal year 1969 cut to be administered in the same way would have been in direct conflict with the purpose of the new management system. The power of the federal government to apply sanctions to noncomplying states would be neutralized.

After much discussion, ICESA agreed that selective cutting could be used, but demanded that the federal government tell the states where and how to do so. It was hoped that assumption of responsibility by the federal government for decreases which were sure to be unpopular with some elements of the employment service constituency would relieve the pressure on state agencies and make the whole operation, if not pleasant, at least palatable.

With this support from the Interstate Conference, the Manpower Administration moved ahead to use the state plans of service as the basis for implementing the budget cut. In October 1968, the U.S. Employment Service sent out detailed instructions to the states listing those activities which should or could be curtailed, and telling them how funds could be shifted around in order to absorb the cut.[10] Chief among the activities that states were directed to put in a low priority status were those being provided to

[10] U.S. Department of Labor, Manpower Administration, Bureau of Employment Security, General Administration Letter, No. 124, October 18, 1968.

35

job-ready applicants. Professional applicants were to be encouraged to make use of self-service information aids. Such activities as the nurse's registry, teacher placement, and convention placement services were to be cut. The use of counseling and testing staff for non-disadvantaged applicants was to be kept to a minimum. The cooperative school program was to be redirected to serve those young people who really needed such assistance. Casual labor offices were to be closed. Youth Opportunity Centers were to be consolidated with Adult Opportunity Centers. Administrative paper work was to be reviewed and reduced wherever possible.

Despite some residual opposition within the Bureau of Employment Security, the plans of service were used as a basis for decision, and the cuts were made selectively. This represented a real breakthrough in overcoming one of the most difficult problems in the administration of a federal-state program—how to assure effective federal direction without emasculating the role of the states.

Although the plan of service concept has the potential for providing strong federal direction to employment service operations, old methods resist change, and, unfortunately, budget and finance people seem to be among the least susceptible to easy acceptance of new methods. If the plan of service is added to an existing system that continues without substantial change, the result will be nothing more than burdensome and counterproductive paperwork. In government the tendency is for important activity and decision-making to take place at the margin of the budget process. Too often the only significant struggles concern incremental increases or supplemental budget requests. The base figures go unchallenged and pass beyond control. The margin becomes the contested prize. To forestall this in the employment service, all of the elements of the new management system must be put in place and coordinated without further delay. Most important, the people who are involved in the planning, budget, and allocation process must understand the plan of service and know how to use it as a management tool.

STATE MERIT SYSTEMS

It may seem ironic to include state merit systems in a discussion of barriers to change, since it is unfortunately true that these systems, set up with such hope in the thirties as the reformers' panacea, have themselves become formidable obstacles to government reform and social change. There are two major problems with the state civil service systems: (1) the financial problem, the inadequacy of present salary levels; and (2) the problem of personnel administration, including rigid classifications, inappropriate selection policies and procedures, and unimaginative or non-existent staff-development practices.

Employment Service Salaries Today

The one thing on which both critics and supporters of the employment service generally agree is that the salary structure of state agencies is too low to attract and hold good people. But no one has been able, or perhaps willing, to do anything about it. A look at the existing system will indicate why.

Personnel administration of state employment security agencies is controlled by a provision of the Social Security Act which requires each state agency to establish and maintain a merit system; that is, a classification and compensation system for all positions not specifically exempt. The system must conform to standards set by the Secretary of Labor, but each state has final authority for levels and rates of pay in its own system.

There are two principles which the federal government tries to get the states to follow in the administration of merit systems: (1) the principle of internal consistency—that federally grant-aided employees in a state should have the same salaries as non-federally aided employees, and (2) the principle of external consistency—that salaries should also be comparable with salaries in the non-government labor market for similar types of work. The first principle has often worked to the detriment of the employment service, tending to keep salaries down in order to keep them in line with other state agencies; and the second principle has never been pursued with serious intent.

In 1969, there were approximately 67,000 persons employed full-time in state employment security agencies, but they made up only about 4 percent of all state government employees. How does this 4 percent compare with the others and what was their status in comparison with persons in similar occupations in non-governmental jobs? Despite the significant improvement in state employment service salaries, which between 1964 and 1969 increased from 30 to 35 percent for interviewers and counselors, the salaries for these groups—the backbone of employment service staff— are still not competitive with salaries for comparable work in either the public or the private sector.[11] Table 4 compares 1969 salary levels for counseling and interviewing work in and out of government. The classifications selected for comparison are drawn from surveys conducted on a regular basis by the Department of Health, Education, and Welfare (HEW) and recognized professional groups. Insofar as possible, the skill levels, educational requirements, and responsibilities of the selected positions are comparable.

Not only do salary levels for employment service counselors lag behind those of counselors in state vocational rehabilitation agencies, but when compared to the salaries of vocational guidance counselors in school systems, or salaries paid for similar work to counselors employed by the Jewish Vocational Service, a private non-profit agency, it is apparent that the employment service comes out a poor fourth. Employment service interviewers compare favorably with caseworkers in state welfare agencies, but not with personnel interviewers in private industry.

One disturbing development is that although the gap has been

---

[11] Annual surveys made by the Department of Health, Education, and Welfare, Office of State Merit Systems, show that between 1964 and 1969 salaries for employment service interviewers increased 31 percent at the minimum level and 35 percent at the maximum; 30 percent for employment service counselors at both levels. For vocational rehabilitation counselors the increases ranged from 24 percent at the minimum level to 36 percent at the maximum.

Table 4. Comparative Salary Levels for Employment Counselors and Employment Interviewers in Public and Private Sectors,[a] **1968–69**

	Counselors	Interviewers
Employment service[b]		
Minimum	$ 6,930	$ 5,990
Maximum	8,760	7,566
State vocational rehabilitation		
Minimum	7,170	
Maximum	9,417	
State public assistance caseworker[b]		
Minimum		5,746
Maximum		7,560
School system vocational guidance[c]		
Minimum	9,955	
Maximum	11,523	
Jewish Vocational Service[d]		
Minimum	8,400[e]	
Maximum	12,000[e]	
Private industry[f]		
Minimum		7,700
Maximum		10,700

[a] All figures represent median of the range.

[b] "State Salary Ranges," Office of State Merit Systems, Department of Health, Education, and Welfare, January 1, 1969.

[c] "Salary Schedule Provisions for Full-Time Guidance Counselors, 1968–69," NEA Research Memo, National Education Association, July 1969.

[d] "1969 Salary and Personnel Practices Survey of Executive, Professional, and Semi-Professional Staff in Jewish Vocational Services Agencies." Mimeographed material prepared by the Jewish Occupational Council.

[e] Salary for holders of a master's degree.

[f] "Administrative and Technical Report," Executive Compensation Service, American Management Association, 1968.

narrowed over the past five years between the minimum salaries paid to counselors by the employment service and vocational rehabilitation, both of which recruit from the same sources, it has widened at the upper level between the two groups (Table 5).

What this means is that while the employment service may be gradually getting itself into a competitive position to attract young college graduates to entry-level jobs, it will not be able to retain the new staff for long.

That ES turnover is exceptionally high, particularly among

39

Table 5. Comparison of State Employment Service and Vocational Rehabilitation Counselor Salaries, 1964–69 *(in dollars)*

	1964	1969
ES counselor		
Mean minimum	5,346	6,930
Mean maximum	6,727	8,760
Vocational rehabilitation counselor		
Mean minimum	5,791	7,170
Mean maximum	7,269	9,917

SOURCE: HEW.

young interviewers, counselors, and counselor aides is borne out by reports from all parts of the country. Reports—like the one from the area manager of the Boston office—of 100 percent annual turnover among counselors are not unusual.

Although there is no question that it is an important factor, particularly beyond the entry-level grades, salary is not the only issue involved in the high turnover of employment service personnel. Some of the turnover appears to be due to mediocre or poor middle management and supervisory staff.

One positive indication that the employment service is changing is that young, enthusiastic college graduates are coming into state agencies at the entry level, eager to do something constructive about poverty and the problems of urban decay and believing that the employment service offers them an opportunity to make a significant social contribution.[12] This may be especially true of white college graduates, who are often not as welcome in community action agencies and other anti-poverty agencies as blacks.

Unfortunately the young graduates often find themselves enmeshed in a rigid and stultified bureaucracy that erodes enthusiasm and vitiates their efforts. The opposition they meet is characterized more by lethargy and ennui, than by positive actions

[12] No systematic survey has been taken by the authors, but conversations with employment service personnel as well as with young poverty workers bear this out.

40

of resistance. But whatever form it takes, it has a deadly effect —the newcomers are soon looking around for a better place to work, where job satisfactions are easier to come by.

If this problem, which is serious and pervasive, is to be solved, in addition to improving salary levels for the middle management and supervisory personnel, other possible solutions must be explored. They should include better training programs (which will be discussed in the following section), as well as consideration of early retirement plans for those who cannot change.

The Principle of Internal Consistency

When the principle of internal consistency—that employment service salaries should be comparable with salaries of other state government agencies—is strictly applied, it appears that state employment service agencies are not doing so badly. In 1966, for example, the average weekly earning for employees of employment security agencies was 13 percent higher than the earnings of state employees generally. By 1968, although the employment security agency was still ahead, with average weekly earnings of $131.04 compared to $123.46 for other state agencies, this was only a 6 percent difference.[13]

Since state government salaries are already notoriously low, the small advantage that employment security agencies have over other state functions is no reason to cheer. Being a little bit better than the bottom is obviously not very good and certainly not good enough to attract and hold quality counselors, interviewers, and supervisors who make up the vital core around which the employment service must build its functional capability.

[13] The employment security agency figures are derived from the Bureau of Employment Services fiscal year 1969 budget presentation, based on average annual positions and related annual personal services costs for fiscal year 1968. Figures for full-time state government employees are derived from the U.S. Department of Commerce *Statistical Abstract, 1968*, and were computed from average monthly earnings for full-time employees of all state functions other than education.

Although state employment security agencies receive all their funds from the federal government and therefore could be expected to pay higher salaries than other state and local government agencies that are not fully federally supported, this has not occurred to any extent. The employment security program is the only grant-in-aid program in which states do not have to put up a matching share of the total cost.[14] In all other grant-in-aid programs, the states must contribute a percentage which ranges from 10 to 75 percent of the total cost. This being the case, it is not surprising that state legislators—never especially noted for fiscal courage—look with a jaundiced eye at proposals to increase the salary level for the employment service. Even though the increase might be made at no cost to the state treasury, they are justifiably concerned that a raise in the salary level of one state agency could create additional pressure for raising the levels in other state programs, which would cost the state money and put additional strain on chronically insufficient state resources.

It is clear that application of the principle of internal consistency has not produced the desired results, and in fact has worked to hold employment service salaries down to the lowest common denominator. Just how low that is is demonstrated by a comparison of state agency salaries with the standard cost of living budgets for urban areas.

In 1968, an employment service interviewer—a job that requires either a high school education plus experience or a college degree—earned $2,000 less than it took to support a family of four at a moderate level—and this occurred when he was at the top of the scale. The Bureau of Labor Statistics (BLS) "moderate" cost of living budget for a family of four for 1968 was $9,728. The average mean maximum salary for an employment service interviewer in the same year was $7,471. In New York

[14] Grant-in-aid programs are those public programs carried out by state and local governments with federal financial support. The National Guard is a possible exception to the statement that the employment service is the only grant-in-aid program with 100 percent federal financing, but it is not usually considered to be among such programs.

and California, both considered good states in terms of salaries, the top levels were $8,950 and $8,520, respectively, considerably less than the moderate cost of living budget.

The picture becomes bleaker when one looks at the top salary for employment service counselors—a job that requires a college degree plus (usually) at least thirty hours of graduate work, plus some experience in counseling. When a comparison is made between the 1968 mean maximum salary of $8,573 for counselors and the BLS "higher" cost of living budget for a family of four of $14,069, there is a $5,500 gap.

The principle of external consistency—comparability of employment security salaries to those paid for the same type of work in either the private or public sector—has not yet been given a fair trial. However, if it is to be applied to employment security agencies, it must be with recognition that other grant-in-aid programs will have to follow suit. If salaries are to be raised substantially in one state agency, they must be raised in all. Moreover, the federal government must be prepared to make up the difference to the states in the cost. At the present time, the states cannot produce the additional resources necessary to pay their full share of the increased program cost which is the inevitable result of improving salary standards. Unless the federal government is willing to shoulder this responsibility, neither the internal or external consistency principles can have much meaning.

Efforts to Improve Employment Service Salaries

During the summer of 1964, a select committee of the House Committee on Education and Labor conducted lengthy hearings on the employment service's role in the new social programs. A constant theme throughout eight hundred pages of testimony concerned salary levels and what to do about them. However, aside from general suggestions that position classifications should be revised and specifications upgraded, very little was said that was immediately helpful in solving the problem. The 1964 Shultz task force also devoted considerable time and effort to the question of salaries. Its recommendations, which were broad in concept and specific in application, later became the basis for some of the legislative proposals debated by Congress in 1966 and 1967.

The task force outlined the essential steps to make salaries more attractive and more competitive. These steps included full use of his authority to set standards by the Secretary of Labor, rigorous application of the principle of external consistency, a public review panel to follow up on state implementation of federal standards, and the establishment of a new federal Civil Service category, under which college graduates would be recruited for federal employment but assigned to state and local governments for a two-year training period.

The Administration-backed Manpower Services Act of 1966 would have carried out the major recommendations of the task force, particularly in spelling out the authority of the Secretary of Labor to set personnel and salary standards, and providing for the training and exchange of federal and state personnel. However, when amendments were added on the Senate floor by Senator Prouty of Vermont deleting the language on federal standards for state salary schedules and leaving it up to the states to set standards "adequate to attract qualified personnel," the bill lost its power, and, along with that, its Administration support. When it was later allowed to die in the House Committee, it was not mourned by many.

The Administration submitted a new Employment Service Act the next year, but the Prouty message had gotten across. Although there was a reference to the need to adopt a policy governing salary scales, just who should adopt the policy or how it should be enforced was left out. This bill languished in committee for two years. Since it did not tackle this crucial issue there was no effective force behind it. In addition, other Manpower legislation demanded priority attention. The Economic Opportunity Act Amendments of 1967, the Social Security Amendments of 1967, and the Manpower Development and Training Act Amendments of 1968, all took precedence over the Employment Service Act.

44

STAFF DEVELOPMENT

As national manpower policy shifted emphasis to assisting the disadvantaged, the employment service was faced with a triple dilemma in its staff development programs: to upgrade its staff structure; recruit minority groups; and train and retrain personnel for new responsibilities.

To meet the need for counselors and other professional personnel for the new manpower and poverty programs, the employment service had to improve its competitive bargaining position. This meant upgrading staff by establishing higher qualifications and more rigorous definitions of job classifications, particularly in the counseling area. With strong support from the American Personnel and Guidance Association, states were urged to adopt new federal standards which required ES counselors to have a master's degree in counseling or in a related field if supplemented by experience. It was hoped this would enhance the reputation of the employment service within the counseling profession and thus attract the best qualified candidates to work in the new programs.

At the same time, there had to be some way of attracting minority groups into the employment service. The widespread distrust of the employment service which had developed over a period of years, especially in urban ghettos, could not be dispelled without a positive demonstration of change in the hiring and promotion practices of the employment service. To encourage greater utilization of ES by the disadvantaged, more representatives of the target groups had to be brought into the system. Establishment of credibility with minority groups meant this effort could not be limited to low-level jobs, but had to permit full utilization of the special abilities of the disadvantaged, and provide a ladder for increasingly responsible and remunerative careers in state agencies. To do this there would have to be a relaxation of entry-level qualifications, as well as new job classifications and career ladders especially designed for people who had been denied normal opportunities for professional preparation or career development.

So while there was a necessity to upgrade and professionalize personnel qualifications on the one hand, there was, and is, an equal imperative to revise personnel standards for this special group. To be successful, both efforts had to be supported by integrated training programs to back up the education and experience of the one group, the professionals, so that the national manpower policy and goals were clearly understood, and to fill in the gaps in education and technical knowledge of the other group, the disadvantaged, so that career development could be assured for all. The effort to move in both directions during the past six years has been uneven and somewhat sporadic, but moderately successful.

Improving State Staff Structure

Just as the federal government has the authority under the law to set standards for salary levels, so it can also prescribe classification standards. However, since the only recourse for noncompliance is a complete cut-off of state funds, strict enforcement of standards is not a real possibility. Even if it were possible to make the punishment fit the crime, it is unlikely that the federal government would want to intrude itself into state civil service systems to such a degree.

To upgrade counselor standards, the chief instrument for change has been friendly persuasion, and with good results. By 1969, all states had set up counselor standards that conform in large measure to federal ones. Progress has not been so substantial at the other end of the scale—the restructuring of jobs at the pre-professional level so that new positions can be opened up to minority groups. Guidelines were sent to state agencies in November 1967 suggesting the establishment of three pre-professional classifications: employment aide, employment agent, and coach. Two years later, although forty states had set up such classifications, only 2,000 persons were employed in pre-professional jobs.

In the manpower lexicon, the terms pre-, sub-, and para-professional usually relate to staffing that is representative of the target groups being served. (However, the converse does not hold, that the effort to increase minority staff is limited to the development of pre-professional jobs.) When the Concentrated Employment Programs (CEP) were established, a policy was adopted that at least 50 percent of the CEP staff had to be drawn from the CEP target area. This policy was very effective in gaining the trust and acceptance of CEP by target area residents, but unfortunately it is no longer being enforced.[15]

There is some evidence that minority staffing in the employment service has improved over the past three years (from 12 to 14 percent of the staff of all state agencies), but this is no cause for a relaxation of efforts to make further improvements. The long record of discrimination in the employment service comprises an extra handicap that will take more than normal effort or ordinary achievement to overcome.

State Staff Training

The employment service has always engaged in a continuing program of training both for its regular staff and for new entrants. State agencies' proposed training plans, including an outline of estimated out-service training needs, are an integral part of the annual plan of service. In this context "out-service" means training that takes place outside the normal confines of the state agency, usually at a university. The state estimates are reviewed by a committee of the Interstate Conference of Employment Security Agencies, which, working with federal staff personnel, determines the allotments to be made to the states from the trust fund to carry out approved training programs. Funds are also set aside by the federal government to administer an experimental national training center at Michigan State University and to carry out regional

[15] It is only fair to note that the policy was relaxed somewhat during the Johnson Administration, when former residents of the target area were allowed to be counted against the 50 percent requirement.

training programs. Regional programs are set up when training needs in the states can be met more advantageously for a group than singly. For the most part, states prefer to arrange their own training programs for their own people.

Although no precise breakdown of training is available, it appears that a large portion of trust fund training money has been used each year to upgrade employment service counseling. One source reports that as much as 95 percent of the money is used in this way. This is entirely consistent with the urgent need to improve counseling, but it does leave the lower end of the scale without much support.

The CAUSE Programs

The best known and perhaps most controversial training programs carried out by the Manpower Administration during the sixties were CAUSE (Counselor-Advisor University Summer Education) I and II. The first CAUSE took place during the summer of 1964, the second the next year. Both were designed to bring into the employment service a new, fresh, energetic supply of potential counselors to staff the new Youth Opportunity Centers as either counselor aides or youth advisors. Once in the employment service, additional training was to be provided to allow the newcomers to move into vitally needed professional counseling positions.

Both CAUSE programs were conducted on a "crash" basis. Recruitment and selection of the counselor trainees, curriculum development, training objectives, and the like were provided by the federal government. College graduates and non-college graduates over 21 who "feel deeply about the problems of disadvantaged youth" were urged to apply.[16] The training itself took place at more than two dozen universities operating under contract with the federal government. Employment after training was the responsibility of the state agencies, who were asked to set up new

[16] Statement of Secretary of Labor Willard Wirtz announcing the program, June 1964.

48

youth advisor and counselor aide classifications to accommodate CAUSE trainees. To assure utilization of the trainees, authority for new positions for the YOCs was made contingent on the establishment of such classifications. More than 3,300 people were trained to work with the disadvantaged in the two CAUSE programs: 70 percent were placed with state agencies and, of the remainder, 80 percent found jobs in other poverty agencies.

Throughout the program, there was opposition to federal involvement in what had been traditionally a state function. However, most state agencies now recognize that CAUSE produced good people who brought with them a much needed burst of energy, concern, and understanding of the new mission the ES was being asked to undertake.

The CAUSE trainees were not disadvantaged: nor were they intended to be. In the first year almost all of the trainees were white college graduates with previous professional or managerial experience. Even in the youth advisor class—a position that did not call for a college degree—most of the trainees had had two years of college. In CAUSE II, greater emphasis was put on the youth advisors. Special efforts were made to recruit minority candidates, but the program was still predominantly white.

After two summers of concentrated effort, CAUSE was put aside. As an experimental program it had served its purpose. The lessons learned could be put to use by the states if they so desired. To a large extent, most of the states have. Counselor trainee classifications have been established in all states. Many states have also instituted positive programs of recruitment of recent college graduates who are subsequently subsidized at recognized universities for a year of graduate work in counseling.

TIMS—An Attempt to Stimulate the Use of Pre-professionals

The problem of recruitment and training of pre-professionals is still largely unsolved. The attempt by the Manpower Administration to promote such a program in 1968 illustrates the complexities of the training problem and demonstrates the need for strong federal direction and control of ES training.

In the early spring of 1968, the Manpower Administration set aside funds to encourage the states to recruit and train sub-professionals and other professional staff for the new manpower programs. The Work Incentive Program was to become operative in all states on July 1: sixty new Concentrated Employment Programs were in the process of development and the ES Human Resources Development Program was getting underway. All three programs required a different kind of staff than ES had had before, especially coaches and out-reach workers. These are sub-professional jobs requiring sensitivity to the disadvantaged and understanding of their special needs and problems—to be filled, if possible, by persons with backgrounds similar to the client groups. Since the employment service was slated to have a large role in all three programs, the funds were to be used to initiate a training program to assure that the states had the staff for these new manpower programs when and as they needed it.

The program was labeled "Training in Manpower Services" (TIMS). It required four weeks of classroom instruction at a university during the summer followed by four weeks of on-the-job training in a state agency. Unlike CAUSE, the states were to select trainees, contract with universities, and oversee the training operations.

The most difficult problem in getting TIMS launched was the chronic question of positions. In CAUSE, new positions for the Youth Opportunity Centers were authorized before the training program started. Moreover, employment of the CAUSE trainees was a condition for authorization of positions. As a general rule, when it comes to hiring additional personnel, state agencies are an extremely cautious lot. It is not unusual for state agencies to operate with a 10 percent vacancy rate, out of fear that a capricious Congress or the "unpredictable" federal agencies which provide at least half of the money for most state jobs will renege on their rosy promises and leave the states "holding the bag" or force them into dreaded reductions in force. Even though assurances were given for the TIMS program that new positions for CEP and WIN would be forthcoming, without certain knowledge of the amount of money available for the year, the states were unwilling to move ahead.

There were also serious technical problems. For example, many state merit system agencies demurred at the guidelines for pre-professional jobs, prescribing the elimination of written, competitive tests for selection of candidates. Since written examinations are the heart and soul of merit systems, the states' reluctance was not surprising. Another example: The decision to tie TIMS to universities, whatever its value in insuring high quality training, resulted in the insistence by HEW that the state vocational education agencies should have approval authority for individual state projects—a procedural problem that resulted in intolerable delays.

The final results of TIMS were hardly impressive. When the program closed, 325 persons—two-thirds of them pre-professionals—had been trained in seven programs in six states and the District of Columbia. Only 5 percent of the funds originally set aside had been spent.

The TIMS fiasco clearly demonstrates that left alone the states cannot and will not undertake the extensive training job that is necessary either to change attitudes of the existing staff or, more important, to bring about a complete metamorphosis in the character and composition of the federal-state system. The problems that arose in TIMS over eligibility, training standards, utilization of funds, approval procedures, and even employment outcomes were difficult and certainly did not admit to simplistic solutions. But if there had been a strong and clear commitment on the part of the individual states or the Bureau of Employment Security, these problems could have been overcome. The point is that no one *wanted* to solve them and, in the end, they became excuses for inaction, not legitimate, administrative problems demanding solution. Although the misfortunes that befell this program were probably not deliberately induced, the instinct of the bureaucracy for self-protection and self-preservation—whetted by the imminent and certain change in political administrations—proved stronger than the administrative techniques available to the top command.

TIMS is now defunct, but the need for training, particularly of pre-professionals, continues. If anything, it is greater than before. As the WIN program grows or is superceded by the open-ended Family Assistance Plan, and as the employment service comes to rely more and more on the team concept of employability development, the need for coaches, aides, out-reach workers, etc., will increase. Without a centrally directed and controlled effort by the federal government to train new ES staff and redirect the thinking and attitudes of the old, the team concept and employability development model that is now being relied upon to revitalize the employment service cannot get off the ground.

The Interstate Conference of Employment Security Agencies

Thus far, the barriers to change that have been discussed have been internal ones, related to long-established patterns of operation within the employment service or to basic conceptual contradictions. The barrier presented by the Interstate Conference of Employment Security Agencies, however, is entirely external to the federal-state system.

Unlike other institutions whose proprietary interest in the *status quo* and antipathy to change are acquired only gradually and without specific intention or design, the Interstate Conference is an impediment to change precisely because it exists as a haven for those who want it to be a barrier. Taking a stubborn stance of unremitting opposition to almost any suggestion for change, the Interstate Conference offers protective cover for those who would use the employment service to prevent change instead of making it a positive instrument for social reform.

The Interstate Conference of Employment Security Agencies was established in 1937 by a group of state employment security administrators who felt a need to meet on a regular basis to exchange information and discuss mutual problems in the implementation and administration of the new law. It began as a simple, mechanistic, non-political organization to help state administrators iron out administrative details as they overran state boundaries. As time went on the organization changed both in character and in function. It became more formal in structure and more formidable as a political force to be reckoned with.

Affiliation with the ICESA is an agency affair, not a personal one. However, it is the state administrator who attends meetings and conferences. Although other delegates also attend, the state administrator selects them. Only rarely are the three votes allowed each state not cast unanimously.

An executive committee oversees most of the work of the conference. It is supported by a dozen or more standing committees, as well as special *ad hoc* committees that are called into action whenever the federal government suggests some kind of change in the employment security system. Some committees fill a purely advisory role, but others, like the Committee on Training, exercise considerable authority, even going so far as to review and recommend approval of proposals for the expenditure of funds.

The daily work of the conference is carried on by an Executive Secretary, who, although he is responsible to the ICESA, is on the federal payroll, under Civil Service. His office and staff are provided by the federal government and located in the Manpower Administration of the Department of Labor. The special relationship that this officer—a federal employee—has to the Interstate Conference was dramatically brought out during the Senate hearings on the Administration's unemployment insurance bill in 1966.[17]

At one point in the hearings, the president of the Interstate Conference was asked to identify the states which had reservations on the House bill. He said he could not because the poll of the states which had been taken by the Executive Secretary, Mr. Gerald Foster, was secret. Foster was then called to the stand

---

[17] U. S. Congress, Senate Committee on Finance, *Hearings on the Unemployment Insurance Amendments of 1966*, 89th Congress, 2nd Session, pp. 145–46.

and queried by Senators Douglas of Illinois and Hartke of Indiana.

Senator Douglas: May I ask if [your] pledge to secrecy is a federal pledge or a pledge which you took on becoming secretary of this association?

Mr. Foster: It is an understanding I had, Senator Douglas, when I became secretary of the association.

Senator Douglas: Who told you that?

Mr. Foster: This is in our conference constitution and code, sir.

Senator Douglas: Our, when you say "our," do you mean the Department of Labor or the association?

Mr. Foster: I mean in the conference constitution and code.

Senator Douglas: Who pays your salary?

Mr. Foster: The Department of Labor, the Bureau of Employment Security.

Senator Douglas: To whom do you owe allegiance, the Department of Labor and hence to the people of the United States, or to the Conference?

Mr. Foster: Senator Douglas, I work as an employee of the Department of Labor . . . but I am assigned, with the full consent of the Department, as the Secretary of the Interstate Conference . . . .

Senator Hartke: Do you feel that you could not in good conscience tell us the information which I have been asking here in regard to the breakdown on what states voted in what fashion?

Mr. Foster: I could not in good conscience reveal that information, Senator Hartke. . . . The secretary of the Conference has been provided by the Department of Labor since the existence of the Conference.

Senator Hartke: I did not raise that question. I raised the question as to whether or not you are going to take your orders from the Conference or whether you are going to take them from the federal government. . . .

Senator Douglas: Now, I agree with Senator Hartke, if this is your conscience, we will not push it, but it is an extraordinary situation, and either you or the Department have allowed yourselves to be put in a position where you hold yourself responsible to a body other than the federal government of which you are an employee.[18]

The ICESA is unique. No other federally supported domestic

[18] After this incident, Secretary Willard Wirtz issued orders that under no circumstances would facilities of the Labor Department be permitted to be used to conduct any secret polls.

program has a pressure group that is so closely tied to the federal bureaucracy and, in fact, paid for by the federal government. How effective it is in blocking change is seen in the failure of the Johnson Administration to obtain passage of its proposal for reform of the unemployment insurance system in 1966.

A special meeting of the Interstate Conference was held in Phoenix, Arizona, in January of that year, to develop a unified position on unemployment insurance legislation. There was no opposition to the Administration proposals for an increased tax base, an increase in the net federal tax, extended benefits for recession periods, and broader coverage. The tough issue was federal benefit standards. Nevertheless, after considerable discussion the conference voted by a fair margin to support federal benefit standards, requiring payment of benefits of 50 percent of the claimant's average weekly wage up to a maximum of at least 50 percent of the statewide average weekly wage.

When the House Ways and Means Committee went into executive session to write a bill, Chairman Wilbur Mills invited representatives of the Interstate Conference to attend. During the next seven weeks of deliberations a succession of state administrators came in to take a turn representing the Interstate Conference. All of these representatives were men who had voted against the Phoenix position. When the Committee vote was finally taken, federal benefit standards were defeated by a one-vote margin.

At this point the Interstate Conference Executive Committee decided that there should be a new poll, *not* on the standards issue, but on whether or not the House bill, in its entirety, should be supported.[19] Even though the conference was already on record on the standards, this, of course, reopened the whole question.

The results of this secret poll formed the basis of the testimony of the president of the Interstate Conference before the Senate Finance Committee on the unemployment insurance proposals. Reversing the Phoenix decision, he stated that the conference was in favor of the House bill, the bill without federal benefit stand-

[19] Interstate Conference of Employment Security Agencies, *Proceedings,* 30th Annual Meeting, September 26–28, 1966, Gatlinburg, Tenn., pp. 8–9.

ards.[20] Although the Senate-passed bill included benefit standards, it was clear that this provision could not survive in the conference committee. The Department of Labor took the position that no bill was better than one without standards; thus the effort to improve the unemployment compensation system failed. The Interstate Conference proved its ability to thwart change, but it did not have sufficient power to push its own version through Congress without Administration support.[21] The final outcome was a stalemate.

The power and influence of the Interstate Conference is not limited to major issues of legislation or policy determination. Often the Conference intervenes in minor administrative matters as well. The degree of its involvement in day to day operations of manpower affairs is limited only by the willingness of federal officials to recognize and call a halt to the pervasive insinuation of the Conference into routine administrative matters.

The Interstate Conference is something like the U.S. Senate, with seniority respected and firmly in command. The old guard has a tight grip on the conference. It is unusual and difficult for newcomers to influence conference decisions or actions, especially if they differ with the old-timers. The ICESA is a highly political organization which has a potential for filling a very important role—serving as a channel between the states and the federal government. However, as presently constituted, it is not just a channel. It is also a quasi-legislative body, assuming to itself authority over matters which are in the federal administrative jurisdiction. Until a better understanding is arrived at on the role

[20] U. S. Congress, Senate Committee on Finance, *Hearings on the Unemployment Insurance Amendments of 1966*, 89th Congress, 2nd Session, pp. 110ff.

[21] In August 1969, the Nixon Administration presented new proposals for much-needed reforms in the unemployment insurance system, including an increase in the tax base, broader coverage, an increase in the federal tax rate, and other administrative improvements. The new Administration did not tackle the standards issue head on. Except for a generalized warning that if the states did nothing about standards, the federal government would have to, the issue of standards is no further along than it was in 1966.

of the Interstate Conference *vis-à-vis* the federal manpower policy, until the conference is willing to limit its activities to the very necessary and useful ones of advising the federal government on state problems and concerns, it will remain a formidable barrier indeed both to the development of an effective national manpower policy and to the social change which the manpower program seeks to bring about.

3

Signs of Progress

If the barriers to progressive change have been accurately described in the preceding chapter, the ineluctable question is
whether the employment service system deserves to be continued.
We believe that it does. The situation is retrievable; the case for
the continuation and strengthening of the employment service
is persuasive. Three developments in the past few years encourage
confidence in the ability of the employment service to turn itself
around and lend credence to the position that progress, although
difficult, is possible. The three developments are the gradual
acceptance of the Human Resources Development concept, the
introduction of job banks, and the development of neighborhood
manpower service centers.

HRD

Human Resources Development is an elaborate name for a
simple concept—that each person who is disadvantaged needs
to be treated individually and given *all* of the employment assistance he needs to get him to the point where he can compete
successfully in today's job market. Until the establishment of the

new manpower programs of the sixties, it was not possible for the employment service to give each individual all of the employment help he needed. The necessary tools were simply not available. Only with the advent of the new programs could a disadvantaged person be provided with training, work experience, basic education, pre-vocational preparation, and other supportive services to help him move from dependency or a state of congenital unemployment to self-support through a job commensurate with his ability and aptitude. The manpower programs have provided the tools. The HRD program is the means by which these tools can be utilized.

HRD began in 1965 when it became apparent that the Manpower Development and Training Act programs were not getting to those who most needed help. Statistical surveys showed that the unemployed were disproportionately young and uneducated. Teenagers made up 20 percent of the unemployed but only 7 percent of the MDTA trainee group.[1] Also, although 20 percent of the unemployed had completed less than eight years of schooling, only 3 percent of the MDTA enrollees fell into this category.[2]

In an effort to correct this situation and bring more of the disadvantaged into its programs, the Department of Labor initiated the HRD program in four slum neighborhoods in Chicago. State and federal agencies joined together to undertake a program of intensive service to unemployed individuals in those areas. The first step was a door-to-door, person-to-person survey of employment needs in the area. This was followed by a two-pronged effort —working with employers to increase employment opportunities in the area and giving direct help to disadvantaged individuals turned up in the survey to prepare and qualify them for the jobs. The Chicago project was followed by similar experimental programs

[1] Data on teenage unemployment derived from *Statistics on Manpower*, 1969, pp. 12–13. Teenagers include youth aged sixteen through nineteen.

[2] Data on educational status of the unemployed derived from U.S. Bureau of Labor Statistics, *Educational Attainment of Workers*, March 1962, Special Labor Force Report No. 30, prepared by Denis F. Johnston, p. 507. Characteristics of MDTA trainees can be found in *Manpower Report of the President, 1963 and 1964.*

in five other cities to reach out, find, and assist the hard-core unemployed. In August 1966 a directive was issued to all state agencies calling for a redirection of employment service operations to serve the disadvantaged and the establishment of HRD programs in 139 major metropolitan areas.[3]

In the four years following the introduction of HRD, it has evolved from a program of outreach and individual service in a few cities to become the basis for a radical redesign of the structure and operation of the employment service as a whole.

The HRD concept calls for a reorganization of a local employment service office into "employability development teams," each team to give a disadvantaged client the full range of assistance he needs. The team is led by a counselor who is responsible for providing coordination and continuity to all aspects of the client's development. Also included in the team are a job development specialist, a work and training specialist, a coach, and a clerk. All of the team members work *together* to help the client as he moves through the steps of a predetermined plan designed especially to fit his particular needs until he reaches the goal of permanent, suitable employment. A case work approach is used, each team to be limited to a specified number of cases.

Under HRD each disadvantaged individual is assigned to one team which is then required to stay with him until a favorable outcome is finally effected. The responsibility for becoming employable, and for getting and holding a job, no longer rests solely with the individual but is shared by the employability team.

Although this HRD approach has been an employment service goal for at least three years, only in the WIN program has it been given a fair trial. In WIN it is the prescribed *modus operandi* for the welfare clients who are being served. Although this requirement seems to have been honored more in the breach than in the observance, according to 1969 evaluation reports carried out by independent consultants, wherever HRD teams have been put together and used in accordance with the original conception,

[3] U.S. Department of Labor, Bureau of Employment Security, U.S. Employment Service, Program Letter, No. 2092, August 24, 1966.

they function well "more often than not." In fact, despite such problems as initial staffing of full five-man teams, coordination within the team, achievement of the desired caseload ratio, and adherence to the standard requiring continuous contact between the team and the individual, one report stated that "at its best, the team concept works extraordinarily well."[4]

To make the HRD work will take more than the plethora of directives, guidelines, and slick handbooks which have emanated from Washington over the past four years. There must be a determined commitment at the top, backed up by a substantial dose of technical assistance from the federal government to the states, and enforced through a continuous system of federal monitoring and evaluation. It appears that the present Administration has the commitment. A program has been announced which would make HRD the basis for a renewed effort to redirect the employment service system. Whether the federal Manpower Administration can or will deliver the necessary technical assistance and follow-up remains to be seen.

JOB BANKS

The second major development that gives hope for the employment service is the adoption and expansion of the job bank. This is a simple computer system of job market information collected and distributed on a daily basis throughout a metropolitan area. The first job bank was developed in Baltimore, where it has been in operation since the summer of 1968. Under the Baltimore system, job orders from employers are collected centrally and fed into a computer, which turns out a daily print-out of approximately 10,000 jobs. Copies of the print-out are delivered early each morning to about twenty out-stations, located primarily in the central city. Each of the out-stations is staffed by one or two employment service interviewers who use the print-out as a basis for referral

[4] Auerbach Corporation, *Report on WIN Program*, supplement to oral presentation, April 24, 1969.

62

of their clients to jobs. Before making a referral, a call is made to the central office to make sure that the job is still open, thereby protecting employers from an overflow of job seekers and the job seekers from fruitless calls on employers. A regularized system to police the book, using the computer to mail follow-up cards to employers, assures that the job bank is kept up to date.

By making information on the whole gamut of job openings in the area available to the disadvantaged, service to that group has shown marked improvement in the Baltimore experiment. Although total placements have remained about the same, placements of disadvantaged applicants has increased about 250 percent, from less than 20 percent to more than 50 percent of total placements in the area covered by the job bank. By October 1969, the success of the Baltimore system had led to the establishment of job banks in five additional cities, with the promise that 76 would be installed by the end of 1970.

One important feature of the job bank is that the daily print-out is made available to other manpower agencies serving the public. As a result employers are no longer deluged with calls from numerous job developers seeking jobs for their particular clients. According to the Baltimore job bank officials, employers recognized the resulting benefits to their own operations by increasing utilization of the bank.

There are problems with the job bank. We must be careful not to be carried away with the idea that modern technology can provide all the answers to deep-seated social and economic problems. Even in Baltimore, which is highly touted as a successful program, only 70 to 90 placements are made a day—not very impressive considering an area labor force estimated in 1969 at 770,000—370,000 of whom were in the central city where the unemployment rate averaged 4.5 percent.[5] Following the pattern of other cities, it can be assumed that the unemployment rate in the slum areas is at least double and could be triple the rate for the city as a whole.

[5] U.S. Department of Labor, *Manpower Report of the President, 1970,* p. 294.

Much of the success of the job bank in helping the disadvantaged will depend on the skill of the interviewer who is manning the job bank out-station. He must be able to judge when an applicant should be referred to a job in the bank, or when a better course for him would be enrollment in one of the manpower programs. He must be sensitive to the needs and the potential of the individual applicant. There must be assurance that the individual who may not be job-ready gets the assistance he needs in order to move ahead, and is not sloughed off into another menial dead-end job simply because it is there.

A principal purpose of our manpower programs is to provide a skilled and mobile labor force which can take advantage of the job opportunities that are made available. Therefore, there must be an emphasis on employability development as well as on job placement. The employment service must not be allowed to deteriorate into a larger and more widely distributed daily classified ad system, performing essentially the same function as the local newspaper except on a broader scale. As a first step, the bank should include training opportunities as well as job opportunities. At the present time this is not being contemplated except in one or two of the experimental job-matching programs. Outreach will have to be intensified. Counseling will have to be tied closely to the job bank operations. Follow-up must be an integral part of the system. Furthermore, as the job bank is used more and more for self-service for those who are job-ready, care must be taken to make sure that the job bank "book" continues to provide a range of opportunities for the disadvantaged. Jobs that offer good career opportunities for the disadvantaged in terms of training content and upward mobility should be made available to them on a preferential basis.

There is one tangential problem that could assume serious proportions as the job bank is expanded to additional cities. The Baltimore job bank book comprises at least 1,500 pages each day. Some 25 to 30 copies of each daily book are printed and distributed. The books are, of course, obsolete within 24 hours and are replaced by new ones. Obviously, the paperwork involved in the operation of the bank is tremendous. In view of the placement rate of only approximately 70 a day against a job list of about 10,000 openings, the system admittedly has a large degree of built-in waste. It is conceivable that the problem of managing the paper flow could become as difficult as the problem of what to do with the unemployed. In any case, plans to expand the job bank should carefully consider alternative and possibly less wasteful methods of adapting modern computer technology to labor market operations.

Job bank costs vary from city to city, depending on the size of the labor market and the type of system used, but a round-house estimate of the average cost of installation and operation of the mechanical phase of a single job bank is $250,000 a year. The employment service expects to spend approximately $16.5 million on job banks by June 1970 and an additional $31.5 million in the next year.

A logical outgrowth of the job bank system is the development of a computer job-matching system. Under such a system, not only job openings are computerized but also the qualifications, interests, and aptitudes of the job applicant. The two sets of information are fed into a computer system which provides a match. In theory, a job-matching system could comprise any geographical area desired—city, metropolitan area, state, or even the nation. By March 1970, experiments in computerized job-matching systems were being carried out in four states—Wisconsin, Utah, New York, and California—with plans being made for an expansion to fourteen by June 1971. Successful computerized job matching could eliminate the need for job banks and job print-outs, but it requires a degree of technical sophistication that is only beginning to be developed. There is reason to believe, however, that it is a feasible method for the provision of employment services and, moreover, one that can bring about significant improvements in the workings of the labor market. The end result would be the strengthening of the national economy and the advancement of the nation's social objectives *vis-à-vis* the disadvantaged.

Employment Service Staff in Target Neighborhoods

A third sign of progress and change in the employment service is in the utilization of employment service staff in neighborhood manpower service centers. Although there are no overall statistics on the extent of staff out-stationing, numerous examples can be found of employment service staff working in small manpower centers in the slum areas of our major cities, either in cooperation with community action agency staff or alone.

The establishment of the Concentrated Employment Program and the requirement that the employment service be the presumed supplier of manpower services for that program has pushed local employment service agencies into many areas not previously penetrated. Arrangements between the community action agencies, which are generally the sponsors of the Concentrated Employment Programs, and the local ES agencies differ widely in the different CEPs. In some cases, the employment service role is limited to the out-stationing of a few job developers or counselors in a CEP center. In others, the employment service operates one or more centers entirely. In several CEP programs, the employment service is the major subcontractor, providing almost all of the manpower services, and in two CEPs it is the sponsor. While the variations of ES involvement are as extensive as the number of CEPs, in every case, arrangements *have* been made, and there is no CEP where the employment service does not play some role. Revised guidelines issued in 1969 called for an even greater involvement of the employment service in the CEPs, requiring ES assumption of responsibility for all manpower services as a single package.

A good example of an adapting employment service is in the Detroit Concentrated Employment Program sponsored by the Mayor's Committee on Human Resources Development, a community action agency. The Michigan Employment Security Commission (MESC) is the chief subcontractor. The CEP operates from a central office and four in-take centers located in the target area. These centers are part of Detroit's total human resource development program and are administered by the Mayor's Committee on Human Resources Development. The CEP program, although staffed by MESC, operates from these centers. The HRD approach is used in providing assistance to enrollees. There are approximately twenty three-man teams, each consisting of a counselor and interviewer who are state employment service staff, and a para-professional counselor-aide, who is an employee of the city. Job development is centralized in the main office and handled by MESC.

In addition to the CEP operation, MESC has several mobile stations in the central city; stations that can put one or two staff people into store-front operations wherever they are needed. The MESC is also involved in the Detroit Skill Center operated by the state vocational education system. In this case, both job development and placement for the skill center trainees are performed by MESC staff located there.

Increased participation of employment service personnel in the new manpower development programs is one indication of incipient change. Another is the occasional evidence of a growth of understanding of the problems and special needs of the poor among even the old-line established staff. In Boston, for example, where employment service staff are out-stationed in the CEP to work on job development and placement, some of the ES people were initially unsympathetic to the group they were serving. They were used to and expected punctuality, neatness, self-reliance, and conformity to standard work procedures from applicants. However, after working in the CEP center for a time, the employment service staff have changed their attitudes and often find themselves defending their clients against the community action agency staff who want to take a hard line with the enrollees.

Obviously, it is not difficult to find cases where the employment service has been unwilling to change and take responsibility for serving the disadvantaged. In New Hampshire for instance, the state employment service has withdrawn its people from the CEP altogether and insisted on keeping them in the regular office. Other instances of non-cooperation could be mentioned, but the important thing is a beginning has been made. It is a small beginning, but a hopeful one.

4

Alternative Solutions

A comprehensive analysis of the federal-state employment service must consider the possible alternatives to the present system as well as the case for continuation of the *status quo*. Despite the hopeful signs of progress that have been discussed in the previous chapter, examination of other courses must be made.

Federalization is not the key issue here. Whenever federalization has been mentioned—and it has been mentioned periodically since World War II—the result has been an arousing of opposition and a polarization of attitudes. Talk about federalization evokes strong and predictable reactions from many quarters—in Congress, in the states, and in the federal bureaucracy. It is neither necessary nor politic to divert attention from what *is* the key issue, namely, the conversion of the employment service into an effective agent of national manpower policy. If there is agreement on the objectives, then the problems of how to best achieve them can be resolved. Foremost among our objectives must be a reassertion of federal leadership. The bugaboo of federalization must be laid aside.

The Employment Service as an Investment

The basic argument for the continuation of the employment service is always that it represents an investment of money and manpower which can not be lightly tossed aside. President Johnson used to say whenever his critics became especially harsh, "I'm the only President you've got." Much the same thing can be said about the employment service. It *is* the only one we've got.

Leaving out the unemployment insurance aspect of employment security work, in 1969 the ES employed more than 35,000 workers. These people were located in more than 2,200 state and local offices throughout the country.

In the last ten years the amount of money going to the states each year for the operation of the employment service has more than quadrupled (see Table 2). This very sizeable outlay, which the federal government has been making year after year, has totaled over $2 billion since 1961.

Measured in strictly quantitative terms, it must be conceded that this 400 percent increase in the annual federal investment has not been matched by a comparable increase in service. During the same period—1961–70—the number of people who applied to state offices for job help increased only 4 percent, from 10.6 to approximately 11 million. The argument can be made that since the new applicants who come to the employment service offices today may be disadvantaged, the tremendous increase in employment service expenditures is justified because the disadvantaged, being harder to help, take more time as well as more costly professional services, counseling, testing, and the like. No doubt this is true, although it is somewhat discouraging to find that the ratio of counseling interviews per new applicant has increased only slightly over the same ten-year period—from 17 to 22 percent (Table 6).

Equally discouraging is the fact that only 1.6 million of the 11 million new applicants in 1969 were disadvantaged,[1] less than 15 percent of the total.

[1] Statement of George Shultz, Secretary of Labor, before the Subcom-

Table 6. Employment Service Activities, 1961–70 *(in thousands)*

Fiscal Year	New Applications	Counseling Interviews	Interviews as a Percentage of Applicants
1961	10,605	1,783	.17
1962	10,414	2,021	.19
1963	11,046	2,088	.19
1964	10,924	2,008	.18
1965	10,944	2,115	.19
1966	10,626	2,285	.22
1967	10,604	2,114	.20
1968	10,517	2,286	.22
1969[a]	10,717	2,337	.22
1970[a]	11,019	2,437	.22

SOURCE: U.S. Employment Service.
[a] Estimate.

However, the impact of the four-fold increase in expenditures should be measured in qualitative as well as quantitative terms. There are embryonic improvements which must be recognized. Among them are the following: entry level salaries have increased; new personnel classifications have been developed; a new and different kind of staff have begun to come into the employment service; there is some indication of progress in the employment of minority groups; and modern management techniques are being adopted.

One alternative to continued reliance on the employment service is the creation and support of a separate system to provide manpower services to the disadvantaged. Such a course would be both costly and wasteful. First, the legal requirements to continue administering the work test to unemployment insurance claimants and to carry out the purpose of the Wagner-Peyser Act would necessitate the existence of a structure similar to the one we now have. Any new system geared toward serving the disadvantaged would have to be an extra, superimposed on the old. Inevitably, there would be overlap and duplication of function.

Second, and of more consequence, is the problem of proper

mittee on Employment, Manpower and Poverty, of the Senate Committee on Labor and Public Welfare, November 4, 1969.

71

utilization of our scarce manpower expertise. Manpower as an element of human resource development is a relatively new field of social policy. The supply of trained people to work in manpower programs is already pitifully scarce, and, whether we like it or not, much of the existing expertise is now in state employment service agencies.

If a competing system of manpower service centers were established—operated by local governments, community groups, or by federal government itself—some of the present staff of the state agencies would certainly transfer to the new system. Indeed this did occur when new manpower centers were set up under the OEO Community Action Program and the MDTA experimental and demonstration program. The transferees would include the best staff—the most aggressive, energetic, and innovative—particularly if the salary level in the competing system is higher than existing state civil service levels. Both the old and the new systems would have serious staffing gaps, competition would become fierce, and turnover would become worse than it is at present. There is no guarantee that the quality of service would improve. In fact it might deteriorate.

It should also be recognized that the present employment service is not merely a collection of 2,200 local offices. It is a federal-state system in the full meaning of the phrase. It is supported by the not inconsiderable resources and technical capability of the federal government—a capability that could not easily be made available to either a local or a neighborhood system. Moreover, state governments control important resources such as health, education, and economic development that supplement manpower efforts. These resources, which are not usually available to local agencies, increase the importance of the states' role in manpower programs.

General Revenue—An Alternative to Trust Fund Financing

The present system of dependence on the Unemployment Trust Funds for the operation of the employment service has produced as many—and perhaps more—problems than benefits. Undeniably, the present financing system was necessary in the early days of the employment service to encourage the states to join in the program. Without financing from the unemployment tax, it is unlikely that the national federal-state employment system would have ever been sustained. Moreover, after the experience of the war years, when employment service was 100 percent federally financed, it was not really politically feasible to go back to a 50–50 sharing arrangement. Trust fund financing has provided a continuity and stability that was essential to the steady development of the employment service. Today, however, the disadvantages of this system outweigh the advantages.

—*It is inequitable.* No one group should have to bear the burden of a system that is intended to fill a public need, indeed, a public obligation. Employers should not be asked to provide the sole support for a program which is recognized as part of the government's responsibility to all of the people.

—*It makes the employment service hopelessly vulnerable to special interest pressures and gives employers disproportionate influence and control over ES operations.* The fact that employers must foot the bill for all of the operations of the employment service gives that group a vested interest that frequently runs counter to the national interest. Exhortations for financial sacrifice in the name of the public good have never proved effective over a long period of time with business or labor, or, indeed, with any other group. No appeal to employers' better natures can contradict the hard fact that under the present system it is in employers' immediate interest to keep the cost of employment service administration down. Improvement of the employment service is almost impossible if it entails increased spending. Any suggestion to increase employment service expenditures runs into a flurry of opposition, which is not only well organized but also has some justice on its side. This is especially true when the proposed improvements are

73

intended for groups who are not even in the unemployment insurance system.

—*It does not provide adequate funds for the employment service to meet its responsibilities.* The fact that the employment service gets more than 25 percent of its funds from sources other than the Trust Account is evidence of this inadequacy. Even if there were a more efficient deployment of existing employment service staff—for example, by cutting back on some of the traditional operations such as the school testing program, the nurses' registry, and convention services—there is still room for a vast improvement of services to the disadvantaged, both in quantity and quality. Such an improvement would require more money than can be realistically expected from the trust account. Although it is possible to increase the trust account—for example, by raising the taxable wage base—the necessary improvements in the employment service would still cost more money than employers are willing to see used for assistance to workers not covered under the unemployment insurance system.

—*It mitigates against national direction of the system and undermines federal administrative efforts to reassert and retain leadership.* The interrelation between the unemployment insurance tax system and the employment service is such that the issue of state *versus* federal control has never been entirely resolved. As long as the money is collected by the states, there is some basis for the claim made for state control of that money. The system provides protection to the states from a patent obligation to acquiesce to federal decisions. It puts the state agencies in a sheltered position, one degree removed from the scrutiny of Congress and the concomitant requirement that their performance be judged in relation to national objectives.

—*Finally, the system forces the Manpower Administrator to resolve the federal-state conflict in the most difficult and sensitive area*—state taxing systems which are the provinces of fifty state legislatures.

It has long been recognized by most experts (and certainly by harried program administrators) that if the funding problem is to be resolved, there must be supplemental financing from general revenues collected by the U.S. Treasury and appropriated annually by Congress. Provisions in two Administration legislative proposals—the comprehensive Manpower Training Act and the Unemployment Insurance Act—would open the door to general revenue funding.[2] The UI bill would allow costs which are not an appropriate charge to the regular unemployment insurance system to be financed from general revenue. The Manpower Training Act makes specific reference to funds appropriated to the employment service under the Wagner-Peyser Act and provides that such funds be included in the overall state manpower development plan.

It has been argued that to switch from trust fund revenues to general revenues would add to inflationary pressures. However, it is excess aggregate demand evidenced by total federal expenditures that contributes to inflation; the expenditures for the employment service will be made regardless of the source of revenue.[3] While it is theoretically possible that charging all employment service expenditures to general revenues would result in an increase in general taxes, and a consequent increase in the national debt—also a significant inflationary factor—it can be argued persuasively that such a result is not likely to occur. By shifting regular employment service financing to general revenue, the present .4 percent tax on employers could probably be reduced by half, or even more. With an increase in the taxable wage base, the rate could be further reduced.

[2] The Nixon Administration has made the overhaul of manpower legislation a principal goal of its domestic program. During the first year of his Administration, President Nixon proposed a Comprehensive Manpower Training Act and an Unemployment Insurance Act. Congress had not completed action on either proposal by May 1970, although hearings were held and separate versions of the UI Act were passed by both the House and the Senate.

[3] It was in recognition of the importance of the levels of total expenditures that the federal budget concept was changed in 1968 from a balance of new obligational authority (money appropriated annually by

Approximately half of the total amount appropriated from the trust fund account for the administration of the employment service has been used in recent years for carrying out the unemployment insurance system and half for regular employment service operations (see Table 1).

With general revenue financing, only the cost of administering the unemployment insurance system would continue to be financed from the Federal Unemployment Tax Act (FUTA). Services performed by the employment service in connection with unemployment insurance, such as administration of the work test, could be *purchased* by the UI agency from the employment service. Other employment service operations could be financed from an appropriation equal to the .2 percent tax saved, plus whatever additional amounts were necessary to make the employment service an effective operating arm for national manpower policy. With financial responsibility distributed over a larger group, there would be no significant increase in the overall tax burden. Furthermore, the switch from trust fund to general revenue financing would insure that the non-unemployment insurance portion of employment service operations would be accountable to the whole body politic—not just employers. Finally, employers enjoying the benefits of a reduced tax burden would no longer have reason to oppose much needed improvements.

THE CASE AGAINST UNIVERSAL SERVICE

The case against universal service is not so much a philosophical debate as a pragmatic problem in the allocation of resources. Even conceding the broad scope of the Wagner-Peyser Act, as long as resources are limited—which would appear to be the normal situation for the foreseeable future—universal service is not a practical, attainable goal. The urgency of national manpower objectives and the relative scarcity of funds make it imperative to make choices among potential employment service clients.

Congress) against annual general revenues, to a balance of total expenditures (money actually spent each year by the federal government) against all sources of revenue.

It is not a foregone conclusion that redirection and concentration of the employment service effort to certain priority groups will inevitably result in a permanent incapacity to provide service to other groups as the need arises. The contention that once the capacity for comprehensive service to all groups is lost, it is lost forever, assumes an unduly pessimistic view of man's adaptability.

It has been estimated that a worker today will have to change occupations at least five times in his lifetime—so that he must continually acquire new skills. It seems ironic to contend that the employment service which is in the business of retraining and helping workers to adapt to changing occupational patterns cannot successfully retrain its own personnel. It is hard to accept the proposition, for example, that a counselor, used to working with applicants for professional jobs, cannot be trained to work with the disadvantaged—or *vice versa*.

Nor is the problem of local office location insuperable. Increased automation of local employment service operations, with centralized matching of jobs and training opportunities to individual applications, can transform the functions of local offices. No longer dependent for job orders on localized labor markets, and with the broad and diverse range of jobs in the entire labor market area made accessible through high-speed computers, the feasibility of flexible response is greatly increased. Decisions as to the location of small offices within a labor market area can be made in terms of the people who need to be served, not on the peripheral issue of what is convenient for particular kinds of employers. Since the computer enables the employer to be exposed to the broadest possible labor market, he is better served than by any conceivable office location, no matter how conveniently placed it is *vis-à-vis* his work.

The argument that an employer clientele is difficult to develop and therefore must be protected avoids the real issue. The national policy of full employment is not addressed to the needs of employers but to the needs of individual workers. There is nothing inherently wrong with employers using some source other than the employment service to satisfy their labor requirements. The employment service accounts for only 10 to 15 percent of total placements. The fact that this rate of penetration has remained constant over a long period indicates that insofar as employers are concerned the free labor market meets their demands. It is on the supply side that the normal working of the labor market has failed, and where the additional support provided by the employment service is necessary.

One final point must be emphasized. As long as the national manpower goal is the reduction of hard-core unemployment and under-employment, who is to provide the necessary manpower services if the employment service does not? If ES must continue to provide service to all, it cannot adequately serve the disadvantaged given the present resources or even with any conceivable increase in resources.

As a nation, we have resolved the issue of how "public" a public service has to be in other areas of social concern. No one questions that publicly supported medical services should be available to those who cannot afford to pay full price—and not to all. There is no reason why we should not be equally selective with regard to employment services.

ALTERNATIVE SOLUTIONS TO THE SALARY PROBLEM

If the choice is made to retain and strengthen the employment service, resolution of the salary problem becomes imperative. Time is running short. With the best recruits leaving almost as fast as they can be brought in, the time is not far off when the most capable, as they learn about the experiences of those who immediately preceded them, will be discouraged from even applying for ES jobs.

Several alternatives to the problem can be offered. One, of course, would be the federalization of the employment service, with the Federal Civil Service system and standards superceding the state systems. Highly qualified young people would be attracted to employment service careers in greater numbers, and the problem of recruiting minority group members would be alleviated, if not completely resolved. Furthermore, federalization would make easier recruitment of high-caliber middle-level management staff, because of the wider opportunities that exist in the federal service for career development and advancement. However, such a course is not presently a practical solution. Even in an administration less committed than the present one to the decentralization of authority and sharing of responsibility with state and local governments, federalization of the employment service is not a politically feasible alternative.

A second alternative—one that was considered by the Shultz task force—is enforcement of the principle of external consistency, with the federal government giving supplemental grants as a reward to those states that meet high standards. However, this would very likely result in making the rich states richer, while the poor states which could least afford to raise salaries would be put in an even less favorable position.

The third and most desirable alternative is the imposition of federal standards for classification and salary scales for employment service personnel. The Secretary of Labor now has the authority to set such standards and to enforce them by refusing to authorize funds for states which do not measure up. Whether the states can or want to raise salaries in one department but not in others is another problem. It is certain that unless the federal government sets standards, nothing will happen. The argument that states cannot afford to raise salaries because of the pressures they would have to face to equalize pay in other state agencies should not continue to frustrate federal initiative in this area.

There is considerable evidence that state employment security administrators would welcome positive federal action on salary scales, but cannot publicly admit support because of loyalty or delicate regard *vis-à-vis* their governors. It is possible that improvement in employment service salaries could stimulate a general raise in state government pay scales. In the light of the tremendous increase in popular expectations for government services, such a development could only prove beneficial. The present low level of state salaries is not sufficient to attract good personnel to provide the many services demanded. States can no longer afford to remain in a non-competitive position, relying on individual altruism or dedicated selflessness to provide quality performance. They must pay higher salaries. There is no reason why the employment service should not lead the way.

THE EMPLOYMENT SERVICE—THE CHOSEN INSTRUMENT?

During the last months of the Johnson Administration, a little-publicized but prestigious Task Force on the Organization of the Social Services finished its work and made its recommendations to the Secretary of Health, Education, and Welfare, Wilbur Cohen. The task force, chaired by Dean Charles Schottland of Brandeis University, had been asked to develop information and a point of view about the planning and organization of social services, specifically in relation to their priority in our complex and rapidly changing society. Since the task force included job placement and manpower training services within the scope of the social services it was considering, it is worth looking into their recommendations.

A basic principle of group agreement was that the effective delivery of social services must permit free choice by the consumer from different systems of delivery. "Free choice by the consumer should be enhanced, as the enhancement of freedom is fundamental in the United States. However, *services that are monopolized by government or by a single voluntary agency lack stimulus to continuous renewal and improvement.* The consumer should be able to select the agency from which he receives service from two, if not more, possibilities."[4]

This principle is as relevant to the provision of manpower services as it is to other social services. In fact, it may have a special application in the area of employment assistance. Without competition, the disadvantaged individual will be the loser. The chances of his being able to fully develop his employment potential will be reduced since he will have to take whatever is offered. The result could be a negative impact on the economy as

[4] U. S. Department of Health, Education, and Welfare, *Social Services for People*, Report of the Task Force on Organization of Social Services, October 15, 1968, p. 36.

a whole, as we strain to meet the nation's ever-changing manpower needs and as advancing technology forces changes in the job structure.

Without specific intention, the task force report describes correctly the state into which the employment service had fallen in the sixties, particularly in providing services to the disadvantaged. Lacking competition, there was no stimulus to continual renewal and certainly no improvement. However, the necessary revitalizing competition has now been provided through the agencies which have developed as a result of the manpower and anti-poverty programs—primarily, the OEO community action agencies but also the projects established under the MDTA experimental and demonstration program.

The employment service is showing signs of change, but it is evident that it has been pushed there by the competition. Specific instances of the benefits of competition will be useful.

The field of testing has long been one in which the employment service has a well-deserved professional pride. During the forties and fifties, ES was an acknowledged leader in the development of tests that could be used as accurate measures of occupational aptitudes and predictors of vocational success. The employment service was—and still is—often called upon by employers to administer tests to be used as a basis for selection for employment. Yet, when it became evident that the tests were not relevant to the disadvantaged and that, furthermore, they were being used as a screening-out device rather than a *bona fide* selection method, the employment service did *not* seize this opportunity to develop new ones designed to meet the special problems of the disadvantaged. It did not provide the leadership that could justifiably be expected from a public service agency. Instead, leadership fell to other competitive agencies. The Jewish Vocational Service, for example, has developed (albeit with federal support through the experimental and demonstration program of the Manpower Development and Training Act) a work sampling technique that eliminates the cultural bias of standard written aptitude tests. Although this technique has been adopted—not voluntarily, but by federal direction—by state agencies who are now required to include it in both the Work Incentive Program and the Concentrated Employment Program, the status of the employment service as the leader in the testing field has suffered and, along with it, the opportunity to bring about change.

The Manpower Development and Training Act includes special authority for the conduct of experimental and demonstration projects to promote a better understanding of manpower problems and develop new techniques and approaches for their solution. To encourage the employment service to develop its own experimental and demonstration projects, for several years funds were set aside from MDTA for employment service use. Despite this effort to stimulate innovation in the employment service, no new ideas were forthcoming, and in the end reserved funds were returned to the special Experimental and Demonstration Division within the Manpower Administration which had the prime responsibility for these projects.

Such manpower program components as outreach and orientation, accepted today by ES as essential ingredients of programs aimed at the disadvantaged, were not developed by the employment service but through experimental and demonstration programs, by community action agencies, Opportunity Industrialization Centers, and other social service groups.

Competition has been good for the ES. It has led to innovation and the adoption of new techniques. The issue is whether now is the time to limit competition and make the employment service a chosen instrument—the deliverer of manpower services in every local area. *Such a step would be foolhardy. If the ES is to complete its reformation—only barely begun—the threat of competition must be maintained.* It can be maintained if the federal government will reassert its leadership in the federal-state system. The employment service should be the basic instrument of that system, but it should never be allowed to sit back, fat, happy, and secure in the knowledge that it is the sole instrument. How such a policy can be carried out will be discussed in the next chapter.

5

Recommendations for a Dynamic Employment Service

In the previous chapters, we have identified and examined the barriers to progressive development of the employment service. Despite the problems presented, this examination has suggested that change *is* possible and that, furthermore, the employment service has the potential to be the effective nationwide instrumentality for carrying out national manpower policy. However, the general erosion of federal direction and control which has developed over the years has become solidified through a gradual build-up of organizational custom and institutional arrangements. Today in the eyes of many of the people who make up the employment service, resistance to change is synonymous with survival. What has happened in the employment service is mirrored in many of the established institutions in this country. As Robert S. McNamara, former Secretary of Defense, described the process and the problem, "Man is the only creative animal on earth, though paradoxically his resistance to change can be heroically obstinate. He builds institutions in order to preserve past innovations, but in that very act fails to promote the environment for growth of new ones."[1]

[1] Robert S. McNamara, *The Essence of Security: Reflections in Office* (New York: Harper and Row, 1968), p. 107.

Faced with the challenge to change, the employment service, like most institutions, reacts by digging into a defensive position of business as usual, justified on the basis of an outdated *raison d'être* and reinforced by a distrust if not actual dislike of those who are pressing for the change. The recommendations that follow will encourage a reaffirmation of federal leadership so that the employment service will no longer need its protective defenses but can assume its rightful position as a dynamic force for change.

Principles for an Effective Manpower Service System

In describing the kind of organizational arrangements required to carry out a national manpower policy, the term, "manpower service" system is used in preference to "employment service" system.[2] Employment service connotes the existing organization. What is proposed here is an organization that does not now exist, but that can and should. This proposal retains the present employment service structure but suggests modifications that will produce the necessary reforms. An effective manpower service system must be built on these principles.

1. The organization must have a clear purpose understood and accepted by all. There must be agreement as to what it is expected to do, what its mission is, and its relation to national goals. If national goals are changed from time to time, the purpose of the manpower organization must be redefined and priorities rearranged. The principle that national goals are to be accepted and implemented permits no exceptions.

2. Communities wishing to provide manpower services must have freedom of choice. To protect this freedom and thereby maintain vitality in a public manpower service system, the potential for competition must be preserved. One of the greatest problems in

[2] The use of the term "manpower service" is not without its problems and pitfalls. In 1966, the first bill for reforms in the employment service was submitted to Congress; it was titled "the Manpower Service Act." A well-known private employment agency specializing in providing temporary personnel, Manpower Services, Inc., challenged the propriety of this action.

84

trying to set up systems for planning and delivery of social services is that, as policy-makers, we try to structure out stress or competition. But just as competitiveness in business leads to improved productions, so competition in the provision of services leads to better and improved client care. Such competition can come from either the private or public sector, but it is a healthy state of affairs and should be not only tolerated, but cherished. If the public manpower service system gains a monopoly, it will very quickly cease to be responsive to changing social needs. Complete security breeds complete complacency. A dynamic organization, if it is to remain so, is one which must continually look over its shoulder to maintain its foreward position.

3. Implementation of a national manpower policy demands strong federal direction and control of the manpower service system, i.e., a reassertion, reassumption, and retention of federal leadership in the federal-state partnership. This does not mean federalization. A national manpower policy that must rely either on the antiquated and sluggish machinery of fifty state legislatures, or on the capricious enthusiasm of hundreds of independent public or private non-profit agencies, cannot succeed. Today manpower policy is too important to leave to chance. It is no longer the stepchild of economic or social policy. It has come of age and demands the establishment of a dependable system for its implementation.

4. The manpower service system must be responsive to differing local conditions and needs. The advantage of our federal-state system is that it provides for local differences. Its continuation can be justified, however, only if states as well as the federal government recognize their responsibility to maintain a flexible response to differing local conditions within their own borders. No longer can any state claim uniformity within its borders either in social, economic, or demographic conditions. There is no state which does not face problems of urbanization. But cities traditionally have been bypassed by state governments. State manpower agencies must become responsive to the needs of the cities, where the most serious manpower problems are located. This is not to say there are not serious manpower problems in rural America, problems which deserve equal attention to those of the cities. But it is clear that state agencies generally need no extra encouragement in rural affairs.

5. *Although manpower policy has come of age, it cannot be developed or executed in a vacuum.* To be effective it must be closely coordinated with other social and economic development programs—health, education, welfare, and area redevelopment, among others. To this end the manpower service system must be closely coordinated with related service systems.

6. *There must be provision for a continual flow of new talent into the manpower service system.* Dynamism implies a constant process of rejuvenation, an avoidance of the petrification that is endemic to government agencies. "Old line" agencies are the natural enemies of change. Unfortunately, they also seem to be the natural outgrowth of bureaucracy. The quickening pace of obsolescence that is effecting so much in our life also applies to government agencies. A government bureau today begins to qualify for the old line sobriquet after only a few years. The only antidote for this institutional stultification is a constant influx of new people. The manpower service system must encourage this.

7. *The establishment and maintenance of a public manpower service system is a public responsibility.* The benefits of such a system accrue to the whole society, not just a part of it. Therefore, the burden of financial support must be borne by the whole society, not limited to one segment, as is the case now.

Recommendations

Conversion of the employment service into an effective national manpower service system is possible (1) if there is a total commitment of the state, as well as the federal, partner to the national purpose, and (2) if there is a clear understanding that major changes in the present system must be made. There can be no halfway measures which concentrate on altering the image of the employment service but ignore the hard-core problems at the center. What is proposed is not a redirection, but rather a conversion of

86

the existing system into an entirely new and different organization.

These recommendations are arranged in four major groupings. First are those which deal with the basic authorization and structure of the proposed new manpower service system. The second group deals with the issue of federal direction and control. The third group is concerned with the relationship of the federal system to state and local organizations. Finally, the last group tackles the problem of staff development—how to attract and retain the top quality staff which is essential to the development of an effective manpower service system.

Basic Authorization and Structure

1. New authorizing legislation is required. The Wagner-Peyser Act which has provided the legislative base for the employment service system for thirty-seven years is inadequate in at least three important respects.

First, the mandate of the act for universal service makes it difficult to establish service priorities. Although it is possible through administrative action to serve target groups on a preferential basis, lack of a legal requirement for such preferential treatment tends to diminish the force of administrative measures. Since there are many state administrators who do not support the federal position, the law's omission in this regard is serious.

Second, the fact that total withdrawal of financial support to a state is the only sanction available to the federal government makes enforcement of standards of performance impossible. No federal administrator could, or would want to, risk shutting down the entire state employment security system. To even suggest this kind of action is sheer fantasy.

Finally, although Wagner-Peyser does call for a system of universal service, it also singles out certain groups for special treatment. Those groups are the handicapped, veterans, farm workers, and residents of the District of Columbia. Translated into administrative terms, this has meant a separate farm labor service, a separate veterans employment service, special attention to the

87

handicapped (usually referral to vocational rehabilitation), and the operation of the employment service in the District of Columbia as a federal agency. There is no quarrel with the requirement for preferential treatment for veterans. Nor the need for special services for the handicapped. The obligation of the federal government in this regard is clear. However, in view of the decreasing importance of agriculture as a major source of employment in this country, there is reason to question the continuing need for a separate employment service system for farm workers. It is not that the categories presently singled out for preferential treatment under Wagner-Peyser should be eliminated. The point is that the list should be revised and expanded. The statutory priority groups which were perfectly acceptable and reasonable in the early thirties are not reasonable in terms of national manpower policy in the seventies.

These deficiencies cannot be completely corrected without new legislation. An earlier study outlines the principal specifications for new comprehensive manpower legislation.[3] An essential feature of that legislative proposal is the establishment of a federal-state manpower service system responsive to national manpower policy. The study also recommends that the Wagner-Peyser Act be repealed and a new manpower service system authorized under comprehensive manpower legislation.

2. New legislation establishing a federal-state manpower service system must define the goals of national manpower policy. It should clearly spell out the objectives and responsibilities of the manpower service system in relation to those goals. It would necessarily establish priorities and specify the target groups toward which national manpower policy ought to be directed. For the decade ahead, it is clear that, except for the veterans who must

[3] See Ruttenberg and Gutchess, *Manpower Challenge of the 1970s,* Ch. 6. A proposal is made in this chapter for a model manpower planning and delivery system geared to the achievement of national objectives but recognizing both the need for local initiative and control, and the validity of the role of the states. Recommendations for the comprehensive manpower legislation necessary to establish the model system are fully discussed.

be guaranteed a full measure of manpower services, the prime target group must continue to be the disadvantaged.

It has been estimated that there are about 11 million chronically poor people for whom employment could be an escape route from poverty.[4] These are the people who could be helped to get better, more remunerative jobs through a variety of manpower programs. They are the "universe of need," the target group. At any one point in time about 400,000 people are actively enrolled in manpower programs.[5] At least 25 percent of these are needy high school students working part time in the Neighborhood Youth Corps (NYC) in-school program. Another 10 percent, conservatively estimated, are not disadvantaged. To the extent that we rely on manpower policy and programs to achieve our goals of full employment, the elimination of all poverty, and resolution of the structural unemployment problem, it is apparent from these figures that our progress will be slow at best. Even assuming a continuing aggregate demand adequate to sustain a steady economic growth— an assumption which at this writing is uncertain—the pace of our manpower efforts will not produce the desired results for some time to come. Wise public policy therefore demands that we continue our manpower emphasis on the disadvantaged.

The debate over the proper focus of the employment service that raged throughout the sixties is no longer relevant—if indeed it ever was. The argument that the employment service must cultivate the professional and highly skilled job market is a spurious one. In the first place, there are simply not enough resources to do both. A choice has to be made. Secondly, there is no evidence to suggest that employers do actually use the employment service more when they are offered service at all levels in a broad range of occupations. In fact, a look at the record seems to indicate the contrary. When the employment service was assiduously

[4] U.S. Department of Labor, *Manpower Report of the President, 1969*, p. 141.

[5] Summary statistics on the number of persons enrolled in selected manpower programs are compiled and released monthly by the Office of Manpower Management Data Systems, Manpower Administration, U.S. Department of Labor.

improving its image in the late fifties, making strenuous efforts to inject itself into the professional job market as a significant source of supply, the penetration rate was about 10 percent. (The penetration rate is the proportion of the total new hirings made as a result of employment service activity.) In the late sixties, when the employment service was giving less attention to applicants looking for jobs in the professional and highly skilled occupations and claiming for itself a presumptive role as the supplier of manpower services to the disadvantaged, the penetration rate was still approximately 10 percent; no change from the days of emphasis on image (Table 7).

Table 7. **Employment Service Placements, 1961–70**   (*in thousands*)

Fiscal Year	Total	Non-agricultural	Agricultural
1961	14,708	5,902	8,806
1962	15,191	6,725	8,466
1963	13,817	6,581	7,236
1964	12,732	6,281	6,451
1965	11,174	6,473	4,701
1966	10,626	6,493	4,133
1967	10,476	6,331	4,145
1968	10,534	5,934	4,600
1969[a]	10,628	5,528	5,100
1970[a]	10,828	5,628	5,200

[a] Estimated. Figures for 1961–66 from Arnold Nemore and Garth Mangum, *Reorienting the Federal-State Employment Service*, 1968. Figures for 1967–70 from the Budget of the U.S. Government, 1970.

In the light of the assumption that the disadvantaged are harder to place than the clientele the employment service previously pursued, the full implications of this static penetration rate deserve further examination and evaluation. Until such an examination can take place, it would appear that "image" is not as important to the successful operation of the employment service as had once been thought.

3. The manpower service system must be totally financed by appropriations from the general revenues, with the single exception of those services which are purchased by the unemployment insurance system. Employment service reliance on the funding mechanism of the unemployment insurance system has created an institutional inflexibility that thwarts every attempt at change within the system. As discussed in the previous chapter, it is wrong on several counts. It is inequitable, produces inadequate resources, leads to the domination of the employment service by UI, gives employers a preemptive interest in employment service operations, and is an effective counter to federal leadership.

Annual appropriations from general revenues for the operation of a manpower service system is an essential element of any conversion scheme. The inequities of the present system would be alleviated; employers would no longer be forced into an inevitably negative stance toward improvements; the chances for adequate financing would be enhanced, and the way would be open for the effective federal direction of the system.

4. *The two services that make up the employment security system should be administratively separated.* Separation is required both to streamline administration and to eliminate the domination of the ES by UI interests. The break-off of the manpower service system from financial dependence on the unemployment insurance system will pave the way for the administrative separation of the two services. Such a separation would go far toward improving the operations of both systems. No longer saddled with the image of the "unemployment office," the new manpower service system will be better able to recast itself into a manpower *development* organization instead of a manpower supply organization, putting together job-ready people and available jobs. Furthermore, the present domination of the system by individuals whose thinking is influenced either by a lifetime of experience guarding the actuarial assumptions of the unemployment insurance system, or by an allegiance—whether real or supposed—to the employer interests in the community would be overcome. It could be supplanted by fresh leadership, specifically trained in the new field of manpower development, dedicated to manpower rather than insurance goals. It is no accident that the best state employment service systems today are those which have al-

ready made an administrative separation between the two employment security functions.

A reservation must be made here. The present responsibility of the employment service for the administration of the work test for unemployment insurance claimants should continue. This recommendation for separation of the services does not preclude the reimbursement of the manpower service system by the unemployment insurance system for expenses incurred in administering this test.

Achievement of Federal Direction and Leadership

5. The federal government must have authority for an item veto over state expenditures. The present all-or-nothing sanction must be modified. If the Secretary of Labor representing the federal government had selective control over state budgets and expenditures, he could enforce standards of performance and assure that national objectives would be met. The present attempt at administrative control through the plan of service is cumbersome and only sporadically effective. Since the system is still in its infancy, plans of service do not at this point accurately reflect realities of operation. Furthermore, there is no meaningful review by the federal government. Although the plans are passed through the regional manpower administrators to Washington, without definitive criteria to measure them, the federal review process is not much more than a cursory examination for adherence to prescribed form and procedure. To be effective, the review should not be limited to incremental additions to a basic plan, considering only proposed new services and new positions. The entire plan should be open to critical examination each year.

Adoption of the item veto would give the federal government the leverage it needs to assert direction and reaffirm leadership. In recognition of this, the Nixon Administration's proposed Manpower Training Act gives the Secretary of Labor authority for a partial withholding of funds, including those granted to a state under the Wagner-Peyser Act, if he determines that the state is not complying with its approved plan. While this is a commendable move in the right direction, it would be more appropriate, and indeed more effective, as part of a total revision of Wagner-Peyser.

6. *Responsibility for monitoring and evaluation of local manpower programs must remain with the federal government.* Only through a positive program of continuous monitoring and systematic evaluation can national objectives be achieved. Faced with continual pressure to reach and serve more and more people in its programs, the Manpower Administration has been loath to allocate scarce resources to administrative activities such as evaluation, which do not produce immediately demonstrable results. In the fiscal year 1969 manpower budget of the Department of Labor, only .2 percent of the total resources was allocated to evaluation. Sensible exercise of budgetary controls is dependent on a continuous flow of reliable information and sound measurements on which policy decisions can be based. Financial control is of only limited effectiveness without monitoring and evaluation.

Abdication of this responsibility by the federal government, or its delegation to the states, would severely cripple the national manpower effort. A system where each of the fifty states evaluates its own programs is absolutely contradictory to a national manpower policy.

7. *The federal government must provide technical assistance to state and local manpower units on a scale not heretofore contemplated.* It is foolish to expect the existing employment service system to turn itself around overnight. To achieve the necessary revitalization or reformation there must be a much bigger and better program of technical assistance than now exists.

Technical assistance has been entirely inadequate because the federal government has not itself developed the expertise necessary to do a creditable job. If good technical assistance is to be provided, the federal government must move swiftly to bring in, or secure under contract, a better supply of manpower expertise than it has had in the past.

8. *There must be a planned rotation of federal personnel within*

the Manpower Administration. In decentralizing operational authority to the field, great care must be taken to prevent the situation that typifies federal grant programs, where the federal representative develops an allegiance to the state or local agency he is working with, loses his objectivity, and becomes an advocate for the special interests of that agency. This situation was especially pronounced in the now defunct Bureau of Employment Security, where federal directives to the states were frequently "reinterpreted" by federal field personnel in such a way that effective control was vitiated.

The successful opposition by BES to a 1967 Manpower Administration directive making the new positions of regional manpower administrator subject to periodic rotation is illustrative of the enduring ability of the bureaucracy to protect itself and the difficulties in bringing about change. (Claiming that the proposed rotation was contrary to the original conditions of Civil Service appointment, the BES, backed by the Interstate Conference, insisted that there could be no enforced rotation—it had to be on a voluntary basis.)

To correct this situation there must be a carefully planned system of rotation of federal officials. Precedents for such a system are plentiful, both in public service and in private industry. Systematic rotation will increase the federal capability for effective direction. Moreover, by providing an effective method for staff development and career progression, it should also improve the overall quality of the Manpower Administration.

9. The Interstate Conference on Employment Security Agencies must be divested of its federal financial support and assume an independent advisory role. There is no precedent for total financing of an in-house pressure group by the federal government. This situation is not only unique, it is unhealthy. For both the federal government and the states, the present arrangement has tended to shut off an avenue for constructive criticism which might have helped the employment service system maintain its vitality. In addition, the sharing of operating responsibilities with the Interstate Conference has led to an intolerable situation where even the smallest administrative actions are subject to time-consuming procedures that make efficient operation impossible. For the states, federal support of the ICESA has meant a bastardization of their role in the federal-state partnership. Titillated by the taste of power which it has garnered for itself, the ICESA sacrificed its independence in order to support the federal bureaucracy which sustained it. In opposing changes in the employment service system during the sixties, the ICESA was on the *same side* as the Bureau of Employment Security which sheltered it. The ICESA was not fighting the federal government, but only the Manpower Administration which threatened to upset its well-established relationship with the BES.

Relationship of the National Manpower Service System to Local Communities

For the national manpower service system to be responsive to local needs, there must be an integration of planning and delivery systems that does not now exist. These recommendations will assure that the federal-state and local manpower systems are coordinated with maximum local flexibility but without detriment to national policy.

10. The local plan of service must be tied into community manpower plans. There should be established in each city a Comprehensive Manpower Planning Board (CMPB) made up of the mayor or chief elected official (who would be chairman), representatives of the poor, employers, labor, and the schools.[6] The local employment service office manager would be required to fit his plan of service into a local manpower plan prepared by this board. If the ES plan of service was unacceptable to the board, it would not be approved by the federal government and no funds would be provided for the state employment service office in that city for any services, including service to groups other than the disadvantaged. The mayor's Comprehensive Manpower Planning Board would be free to shop elsewhere for the provision of man-

[6] Ruttenberg and Gutchess, *Manpower Challenge of the 1970s.*

95

power services under its plan. Such an arrangement would give the community a freedom of choice in the delivery of manpower services and maintain the threat of competition necessary to keep the state agency on its toes.

Under this system, the employment service would have first chance at control of local manpower operations. It would—and should—have a preferential position as the deliverer of manpower services. However, the right of the community to choose would be protected by giving the mayor and his manpower planning board a powerful veto authority designed to force the state agency into making itself the most attractive supplier of manpower services. There is an innate weakness in this proposal—that is, the willingness of the federal government to support the mayor if he does not choose the state manpower agency. It could be argued that it is unrealistic to expect a normal, mortal Secretary of Labor to have the political courage necessary to side with a mayor against a state agency. But such decisions do occur. It is only the first one that is really difficult.

11. The ES should not be given a preferential claim on sponsorship of local manpower programs. The concept of prime sponsorship of local programs is a good one and should be put into effect as soon as possible. However, it does not compel a monopoly of all local manpower programs. The prime sponsor must be the focal point for executive direction, a channel for federal funds, a central point of accountability, a linking agent for the various components that make up a comprehensive manpower system. Moreover, the prime sponsor must be politically accountable for its actions. The responsibility that government at every level has assumed in the past 10 years in the manpower area for providing jobs and job opportunities requires that the prime sponsor of the local programs be subject to control of the voters. In urban areas this means that the prime sponsor must be an agency of the city government. In Model Cities, it could be the city development agency or its manpower component. In other cities, the sponsor should be an agency of the city but should also be responsible to the Comprehensive Manpower Planning Board.

Actual operations could then follow one of several patterns. The preferable pattern would be assignment of full responsibility for local operations to the local state manpower service agency. This presumes, of course, acceptance by the mayor of the state agency plan of service. The state agency could either supply all of the services itself, or subcontract some components to other local manpower agencies, including the community action agency. Other patterns of operation include the subcontracting by prime sponsors of operational components of the manpower plan to one or more agencies, including the local community action agency.

12. Governors must assume a greater responsibility for the integration of federally supported human development programs within their states. Manpower programs alone will not achieve full employment or provide economic opportunity to everyone who wants to work. Full employment in its broadest sense demands a parallel policy of human development. When manpower is viewed in its social context, the necessity for coordination with related human development programs is clear. The employment problems of the disadvantaged are not limited to a lack of marketable job skills. They include poor health, lack of education, social alienation, different cultural patterns, family problems, and many others. If the task of helping the disadvantaged prepare for and obtain good jobs is to be taken seriously, we must come to grips with the problem of supportive services. Although this is an obvious truism, no one has yet found a satisfactory way to bring the parts of a human resource development program together into a coherent whole. Efforts at the federal level have floundered or failed, largely because no single federal agency has had the power necessary to force the other agencies to relinquish any control over their programs.

Some of the federal efforts are the Neighborhood Service Center program, the Centers for Children and Parents, the Model Cities program, and even the Concentrated Employment Program. The Neighborhood Service Center program, after three years of wrangling, finally got off to a feeble start in a few cities, but has since been absorbed by Model Cities. The proposal for the establishment of Centers for Children and Parents was based on the need to provide broad social, economic, psychological, and physical support to pre-school children. It was therefore designed to provide a variety of social services, including manpower, on a family basis, using a neighborhood child-care center as the focal point. Although there were 36 pilot programs in operation in late 1969, lacking discrete funds of its own, the program is not comprehensive in the sense of the original concept. Model Cities cannot, of course, be labeled a failure, but it has suffered from a seeming inability to persuade other agencies to concede to the Department of Housing and Urban Development any authority for allocation of their own resources. The Concentrated Employment Program, which originally had considerable success in pulling manpower components into a single program, has not been able to obtain supportive services on a voluntary basis. Only when the CEP has purchased the service outright, have such supportive programs as health examinations or day care been available to CEP enrollees.

As long as the chief source of supply of manpower-related supportive services is the grant-in-aid programs, administered with considerable independence by state agencies, the federal government cannot compel integrated delivery. State governors, on the other hand, have this potential. As a rule they can command the agencies that control the supportive programs.

To encourage governors to assume their responsibility to pull human development programs together, they should be given an inducement and made responsible for comprehensive manpower planning for their states. Certain cities designated by the federal government would be excepted from this arrangement to do their own planning. Designated cities could include all of the Model Cities, and perhaps all other cities over 200,000. Governors should be given funds to staff their planning agencies. A governor who is able to coordinate other related human or economic development programs with the manpower program would receive a 5 percent bonus over and above the manpower resources allocated to his state.[7] The ES should be given a preferential status to become the chief supplier of manpower services, not only in the state as a whole, but also in the designated cities. If a governor succeeded in coordinating the human development resources which he had at his command, there would be very little to prevent the state manpower agency from cashing in on its preferential status in every part of the state. A state manpower agency which had ready access to state-controlled supportive services would be in a very strong position in any competition for a local manpower franchise.

Staff Development in the Employment Service

This area presents some of the thorniest barriers to change. Structural or organizational patterns can be shifted. Administrative procedures can be altered with the stroke of a pen. Even in the case of legislation, there is the expectation that our laws should be subject to a constant process of amendment and revision. But to change people, particularly their attitudes and patterns of behavior, is very hard. New skills can be taught to even the slowest students but changing attitudes takes time and patience. Adoption of the following recommendations would permit the development of new personnel policies essential to a dynamic manpower service system.

13. The federal government must exercise its considerable authority and influence to upgrade present employment service salary levels. The employment service cannot do a high-quality job if it cannot attract and hold a high quality of personnel. Salary levels must be made competitive with non-government salary levels for the same kind of work. The principle of internal consistency, keeping employment service salaries in line with other state agencies, does not produce staff quality. In fact, it tends to hold employment service salaries down. Although rarely exercised because of pressure from the states, the Secretary of Labor has the authority under existing legislation to set salary and other per-

[7] *Ibid.*

99

sonnel standards. Since ES is entirely financed by the federal government with no state matching requirement, the Secretary can exercise his authority if he will, and insist on higher standards than presently exist. Determined action by the Secretary of Labor in this important area might give the Secretary of Health, Education, and Welfare the leverage he needs to press for equally high standards in other grant-in-aid programs. If federal agencies acted in concert on this issue, the pressure on the states to improve salary levels for all state agencies concerned with human resource development would be hard to resist.

14. Selection of a local employment service office as the prime deliverer of federally supported manpower services in any local area should be conditional on employment in that office of minority groups and representatives of target groups. The employment service cannot successfully serve the disadvantaged until the present pervasive distrust that exists among this group is dispelled. Until the employment service itself can demonstrate its willingness to hire the disadvantaged in meaningful and responsible jobs, that distrust will remain. Because of testing requirements based on false professionalism, or selection procedures designed more to protect the "ins" than to guarantee quality performance, in many states merit systems work to keep out the minority groups and the disadvantaged. The only way to change these merit systems is to find the sensitive pressure point and apply the pressure. The federal dollars that go into manpower programs provided an appropriate pressure point. If the employment service were financed entirely by general revenues, the pressure would of course be increased. Methodical and systematic application of this kind of pressure would inevitably force a reappraisal of merit system procedures, which in turn could lead to the opening of new opportunities in state and local government for the disadvantaged.

15. The federal government should assist state and local governments in improving personnel administration and providing for more efficient recruiting and training of personnel. The Intergovernmental Personnel Act of 1969, proposed by Senator Edmund Muskie of Maine, would open the way for such federal assistance to state and local governments. It focuses on four basic problems in the public service area—the interchange of federal, state, and local personnel, training programs, the quality of the public service and merit system requirements, and personnel management.

Although many of the activities included in the bill are already permissible under existing legislation, the Muskie bill would provide focus and impetus to present staff development efforts of the various grant-in-aid programs. Activities not presently authorized include provision for an exchange of personnel between the various levels of government, opening up of federal training programs to state and local personnel, and cooperative recruitment and examination arrangements under the leadership of the U.S. Civil Service Commission. However, it is futile to talk about additional federal assistance to the state and local governments without providing the money for such a program. Unless there is adequate funding, assistance will be minimal and the program ineffective.

A federally supported student loan program should be established to encourage qualified young people to enter manpower service careers. Such a program could be modeled after the National Defense Education Act, where undergraduates receive low-interest, long-term loans, a part of which can be excused from repayment as the individual fulfills the implied obligation of the loan and actually works as a teacher for a specified period of years. The Muskie bill includes provision for fellowship aid to individuals who are already state or local government employees wishing to undertake graduate work in order to improve performance and expand ability. It does not provide undergraduate assistance, which could provide the key to better qualified state and local manpower personnel.

16. Consideration should be given to development of early retirement schemes—possibly with federal support—to rejuvenate the supervisory levels of the employment service. Like many of our social institutions, the employment service suffers from personnel policies that reward mediocrity and stifle innovation. All too often the mid-level supervisory staff is totally unreceptive to new methods, new ideas, and new recruits. Many of these people can, of course, be retrained, but not all. It may be necessary to establish early retirement plans if the supervisory level of the employment service is to be successfully strengthened. A special task force or advisory commission should be established to consider this question. Early retirement schemes such as are used by the military and the foreign service could serve as models for the commission's studies and recommendations.

17. A strong program of in-service training of employment service personnel must be established, controlled, and directed by the federal government. The most efficient way to do this would be by means of the establishment of regional training centers to which state personnel would be sent.

Responsibility for technical training in employment service techniques and procedures could be retained by the states, although it should be subject to review and approval by federal authorities. But training aimed at changing attitudes or at developing an understanding of national manpower policy and program goals must remain with the federal government. The German system, in which training responsibility is centralized, has much to commend it.[8] Under that system new employees are in a trainee status for three years, with on-the-job training supplemented by classroom instruction. In addition, supervisory personnel are required to take part in periodic training and retraining courses, normally at centrally directed regional centers. This program of training and career development has resulted in a highly competent and well-respected employment service, capable of recruiting and retaining top-quality staff.

A national manpower program demands a nationally controlled training program. As we have shown, the fifty states left to their own devices are not able to develop and carry out the training programs necessary to support effective implementation of national policy. To expect them to do so is to expect the millenium. On this

[8] Richard A. Lester, *Manpower Planning in a Free Society* (Princeton, N.J.: Princeton University Press, 1966), pp. 101–4.

issue—the establishment of a national manpower service system—
the urgency of the need does not permit waiting for the millenium.

CONCLUSION

A basic assumption of this study, as well as of others in the
series, is that social institutions, being man-made, can be made
to serve man. Although institutions tend to develop a being and
purpose of their own, quite apart from and sometimes antithetical
to the purposes of the men who made them, nevertheless, they
are not immutable. They are vulnerable to a jolting reappraisal.
They can be changed.

Unfortunately, government institutions have developed an almost impregnable screen against criticism. The usual reaction to
criticism, whether constructive or not, is a flood of propaganda,
conceding some validity to the criticism and admitting some room
for improvement, but assuring the public that the situation is well
in hand and that progress is the institution's "most important
product." Words become the accepted method of response. Actions need not follow. A glance through the Annual Manpower
Reports of the President since 1965 confirms that the employment
service is no exception to this practice. Each year the promise of
improvement is there, but each year the criticism remains. Rhetoric
can no longer suffice. Clarence Mitchell, Director of the National
Association for the Advancement of Colored People, testifying
before the House Committee in March 1970 made the point
clear.

So far as the employment service is concerned, its record has been
one of dismal failure to assist persons in need of help in the job
field. We have observed the tactic of many of these officials over the
years. Usually they place in employment the persons who are well
qualified and probably could obtain employment without any help.
The individuals who need additional training or guidance and job
counseling usually become a part of extensive files gathering dust in
local offices. We have been trying to make the employment service
offices more effective in handling manpower programs for the last

103

thirty years. Generally speaking the conditions have not changed much for the better.

In this study we have analyzed the factors which have inhibited change for the last thirty years. If the employment service does not develop a total commitment to change, a commitment that is being demonstrated by some of its more progressive elements, it will atrophy and eventually be passed over in favor of new and different institutions. Currently, the alternatives for the employment service are to begin a transformation now or face transference of manpower responsibilities tomorrow. The employment service can no longer afford to use outdated concepts, ingrained custom, and antiquated procedures as a protective shield. Fortunately, there are indications that it does not want to continue this way. This analysis and these recommendations are made in the belief that the employment service will follow the path already begun and elect to change. Moreover, these recommendations are made with the conviction that such a choice will result in a stronger and better national manpower program of benefit to all.

Glossary

BES	Bureau of Employment Security
BLS	Bureau of Labor Statistics
CAA	Community Action Agency
CAUSE	Counselor-Advisor University Summer Education (a summer training program for employment service counselor aides and youth advisors)
CEP	Concentrated Employment Program
CMPB	Comprehensive Manpower Planning Board
ES	Employment Service
FUTA	Federal Unemployment Tax Act
HEW	Department of Health, Education, and Welfare
HRD	Human Resources Development Program
ICESA	Interstate Conference of Employment Security Agencies
MA	Manpower Administration
MESC	Michigan Employment Security Commission
MDTA	Manpower Development and Training Act
NYC	Neighborhood Youth Corps
OEO	Office of Economic Opportunity
TIMS	Training in Manpower Services
UI	Unemployment Insurance Service
USTES	United States Training and Employment Service
WIN	Work Incentive Program (under the Social Security Act)
YOC	Youth Opportunity Center